JUSTICE AS FIT̶̶

Justice as Fittingness

GEOFFREY CUPIT

CLARENDON PRESS · OXFORD

Oxford University Press, Great Clarendon Street, Oxford OX2 6DP
Oxford New York
Athens Auckland Bangkok Bogotá Buenos Aires Calcutta
Cape Town Chennai Dar es Salaam Delhi Florence Hong Kong Istanbul
Karachi Kuala Lumpur Madras Madrid Melbourne Mexico City Mumbai
Nairobi Paris São Paulo Singapore Taipei Tokyo Toronto Warsaw
and associated companies in
Berlin Ibadan

Oxford is a registered trade mark of Oxford University Press

Published in the United States
by Oxford University Press Inc., New York

British Library Cataloguing in Publication Data
Data available

Library of Congress Cataloging in Publication Data
Cupit, Geoffrey
Justice as fittingness / Geoffrey Cupit
Includes bibliographical references and index.
1. Justice. 2. Appropriateness (Ethics) I. Title
JC578.C84 1996 320'011—dc20 96–26274
ISBN 0–19–823901–7
ISBN 0–19–823862–2 (Pbk.)

Printed in Great Britain
on acid-free paper by
Biddles Ltd.,
Guildford & King's Lynn

For my mother and father,
Betty and Jack Cupit

Acknowledgements

I HAVE incurred many debts in the writing of this book. My greatest is to Peter Morriss, who, for more than a decade has discussed—in correspondence and conversations—numerous versions of these arguments. Without his friendship and hospitality writing this book would have been a good deal less enjoyable than it has been.

My interest in justice was first aroused when, as an undergraduate at Lancaster, I chanced to take a course on political ideas taught by Russell Keat and Geoff Smith. This course—much the high point of my formal education—stimulated an interest which has occupied me for many years, and shows no sign of waning. I am deeply indebted to these two fine teachers.

The book developed from a thesis written for the University of Liverpool. I am grateful to my initial supervisor, Terrell Carver, for his help and encouragement, and particularly for his faith in taking me on in the first place. The SSRC provided a grant which enabled me to begin this study. I have worked on this account of justice whilst employed by the Universities of Bristol, East Asia, and Waikato, and by the Hong Kong Open Learning Institute. I am especially grateful to Don Swift, who, as Principal of the Open College of the University of East Asia, in difficult circumstances developed and preserved an environment in which sustained scholarship was possible.

Many of the arguments I offer here—and others since abandoned—have appeared in papers read at various venues. I am grateful for the advice and comments I have received on these occasions, as well as in many conversations over the years. In particular I am indebted to: John Benson, John Broome, Tom Campbell, Patrick Day, Bob Ewin, Mark Fisher, Laurence Goldstein, Keith Graham, Mane Hajdin, Janet Hutchings, Russell Keat, David Lumsden, Thomas Magnell, Norman Melchert, David Milligan, Tariq Modood, Tim Moore, Adam Morton, Nicholas Nathan, David Neilson, Rob Sale, and Hillel Steiner. An anonymous reader for OUP provided two lots of sound advice; Richard W. Burgh kindly sent me a copy of his doctoral thesis; the support of Jack Vowles ensured that my study leave from Waikato was more productive than it might otherwise have been; and Susie Fung's expeditious preparation of the first typescript enabled me to meet a crucial deadline.

Students at Waikato have been a captive audience on which to try many of these arguments; in some years those taking my graduate course have read and discussed earlier versions of the manuscript. I am grateful to all these students for their comments and suggestions, and particularly to David Choat, Jesse Mulligan, and Shane Stuart.

In Chapters 4, 5, and 7 I have made use of material previously published in 'How Requests (and Promises) Create Obligations', *Philosophical Quarterly*, 44/177 (Oct. 1994), 439–55; 'On the Injustice of Ignoring Entitlements', *Australasian Journal of Philosophy*, 74/2 (June 1996), 313–18; and 'Desert and Responsibility', *Canadian Journal of Philosophy*, 26/1 (Mar. 1996), 83–99.

Prue, Thomas, and (recently) Nicholas have provided (amongst much else) many a welcome antidote to philosophizing, a sense of proportion, and a haven when things have not gone well.

My mother and father made many sacrifices to enable me to study, and first taught me how we should act. This book is for them.

Contents

I

Locating Justice

JUSTICE is a virtue. Those who avoid injustice in their dealings with others are esteemed, and are worthy of that esteem. A society which has just laws and a just division of benefits and burdens is superior to one which does not. But though justice is a virtue, it is not the only virtue. This raises the question: what distinguishes justice from other virtues? What is distinctive about justice? This book is an attempt to answer this question, to give an account of the nature of justice.

I will argue that at the heart of justice is one simple idea, and that all we say about justice is to be understood by reference to this idea. The main task of this first chapter is to introduce this idea, and to locate the notion of justice, that is, to explain where justice stands in relation to other concepts we employ when deciding how we should act. The chapter is largely introductory: I do little to defend the account of justice I want to offer, or to deal with objections. However, at the end of the chapter I indicate briefly how the account of justice I defend applies to comparative justice.

1.1 The Main Idea of Justice as Fittingness

Consider the case of an unfair derogatory judgement. Suppose that I believe you are untrustworthy. When you make me a promise I go out of my way to avoid relying upon you; I warn other people not to rely on you. Now suppose I discover that my belief that you are untrustworthy was based on a misunderstanding. I must admit my mistake and acknowledge that I have done you an injustice.

I want to claim that this example manifests—lays out clearly—the form which all injustice possesses, that it is a transparent case of injustice, to be contrasted with opaque cases which possess, but do not manifest, the form which all injustice takes.[1] To do injustices to people is to treat them as less or lower than they are; to treat them as lacking some status-enhancing attribute which they do not lack, or as possessing some status-reducing attribute they do not possess. The fundamental idea of the account of justice I want to defend, then, is this: an unjust act is an unfitting act; it is an act which fails to accord with the status of the person treated.

The attribute in question in the example—trustworthiness—is a virtue: it is status-affecting. A person who is worthy of trust is superior to one who is not: trustworthiness enhances the status of its possessor. It is because trustworthiness is (or is considered to be) a virtue, that treating a trustworthy person as untrustworthy is (or is considered to be) unjust. If being trustworthy were, like being blonde, not a virtue then my treatment of you as untrustworthy, though it may be inappropriate, would not be unjust. Nor is this relation between injustice and a status-affecting attribute accidental: it appears in all cases of injustice; indeed it is part of the very nature of justice, or so I will argue. (As justice is itself a virtue it is possible to do the just an injustice by treating them as unjust. In this case the status-affecting attribute is the disposition to act justly itself. In most cases of injustice, however, the relevant status-affecting attribute is not, of course, the disposition to be just.)

To act unjustly, then, is to act unfittingly, but to act unfittingly is not necessarily to act unjustly: there are actions which are unfitting but not unjust. We might say of those who show contempt for judges in courts of law—perhaps by refus-

---

[1] Cf. 'The clearest examples of non-comparative injustices are cases of unfair punishments and rewards, merit grading, and derogatory judgements. Of these three kinds of activities, *the third seems the most basic from the point of view of justice* . . .' (Joel Feinberg, 'Noncomparative Justice', in *Rights, Justice, and the Bounds of Liberty* (Princeton, 1980), 268, emphasis added).

ing to stand up, shouting obscenities, and so on—that they treat judges unfittingly, as less than they are, but decline to describe such actions as unjust. We might speak, in such cases, of disrespect. Not all unfitting actions are unjust: unfittingness is the genus, and injustice the species within that genus. Justice is a member of a family of concepts. This raises the question of *which* unfitting acts are unjust. How do unjust acts differ from other types of unfitting act? I take up this question later (1.4).

It may seem that this account of justice is no more than a restatement of the familiar view that to act justly is to treat all according to their due. But these views are not equivalent, and to adopt justice as fittingness is to accept much more than the view that justice is giving to all their due. The difference can be brought out by considering the principles of treating in accordance with entitlement and need. Suppose I appear to be failing to honour a contract we have made, and you go to court; and suppose that the judge has accepted my offer of a bribe and decides against you. You complain that you have been treated unjustly, that you have been denied that to which you are entitled. Certainly you have been denied that which is due to you. But it is by no means obvious that you have been treated unfittingly. To become entitled to something is not to become higher, to be rendered more worthy, to have enhanced status. Why, then, should we suppose that if we are treated as unentitled when we are entitled, we are treated as less than we are?

The same point applies in the case of need. It is held by some that, in appropriate circumstances at least, to act justly requires the allocation of resources according to need. This view poses no problem for the claim that justice is a matter of giving to all their due, for it may be said without impropriety that what is due to people is what they need. But, again, it is not clear that to fail to distribute in accordance with need is to treat anyone unfittingly, for it is not true (or, at least, it is not generally held to be true) that to be in need is a status-affecting attribute. Need does not elevate. But if need is not a status-affecting attribute, it is not clear that we act unfittingly in failing to treat in accordance with need.

The view that justice consists in giving to all their due can accommodate such considerations as entitlements and needs because it is not possible to extract from the formula 'give each their due' any specification of *what* is due to anyone. Justice as fittingness is not accommodating to the same degree. It is, therefore, a much more contentious account of justice. We may agree that justice requires all to receive their due without thereby committing ourselves in any way on the question of *how* what is due is to be determined. The situation is quite different if we adopt justice as fittingness. Once we adopt this account we accept that what is required for justice is determined by what is required if we are to avoid treating people as less (or more) than they are. I do not pretend that this question is always easy to answer, or that a clear and unequivocal answer can always be given. But I do claim that this is how any inquiry into what justice requires must proceed.

1.2 *Two Systems of Practical Reasoning: Status and Value*

Justice is a practical virtue, it is concerned with how we should act. To call an action unjust is to say that, other things being equal at least, it should not have been performed. Nevertheless, there are many ways to act wrongly, and to act unjustly is just one of those ways. In the language of reasons for action we may say that to call an action unjust is to imply that there is a reason (though not necessarily a conclusive reason) why the act should not have been performed. To understand the nature of justice is to understand of which type or types of reason for action it is true that contrary action is unjust.[2]

---

[2] One factor in judging the plausibility of an account of the concept of justice is the extent to which the account makes sense of the fact that to call an action unjust is to imply that there is reason not to perform it. On the face of it this point counts against any suggestion that justice is essentially a matter of producing a particular pattern of distribution. It is implausible to suppose that the mere creation of a pattern can provide a reason for

When people consider how they should act they use many different concepts, have many different concerns. The question arises, then, how these many concepts and concerns are interrelated. Do they form a single coherent system; or is our moral thought fractured, being conducted within different and essentially separate systems? I want to suggest that we operate with at least two distinct systems—systems I will refer to as the status and value systems—and that there is reason to view neither system as reducible to the other.

The fundamental assumption of the status system is that it makes sense to speak of beings or entities as existing on some level, as having some particular status. The idea is that beings and entities can be of higher, equal, or lower status. I shall use the term 'status' quite generally, as a measure of superiority and inferiority—the sense in which it is used when, say, we debate the (moral) status of the foetus or animals, or when we claim that beings which are free, rational, and sentient are superior to those which are not. I shall not be using the term to refer to the 'social estimation of honour'.[3] I shall not be using 'status' in such a way as to define our status by reference to the beliefs or actions of others.

The different status levels in a hierarchy or on a scale are referred to as the grades, ranks, or degrees. Assignment to a particular status is to be made on the basis of status-affecting attributes. These include virtues and vices, merits and demerits, qualities and flaws. The higher may be spoken of as noble, honourable, revered, sacred, holy, reputable, respectable, and dignified; the lower as base, ignoble, unworthy, dishonourable, humble, brutish, undignified, profane, disreputable, depraved, and despicable.

It is sometimes possible for a being or entity to move up or down, to change its level or status. Thus we speak of promoting, dignifying, deifying, ennobling, elevating, consecrating,

---

action—leaving aside aesthetic considerations which are, surely, too weak to form the foundation of justice. To be sure, a particular pattern may result from acting justly; but producing a pattern is not the reason for acting justly.

[3] The phrase is Weber's: see *From Max Weber: Essays in Sociology*, trans. and ed. H. H. Gerth and C. Wright Mills (London, 1970), 187.

and civilizing; and of degrading, relegating, denigrating, debasing, humbling, desecrating, dehumanizing, and barbarizing; of holding down and setting free to rise. We are able to lower ourselves and others; we are capable of self-degradation and humiliation. The notion of self-realization—the achievement of a higher status through the realization of some existing, albeit latent, higher nature—seems to find its home here.[4]

We also speak of treating a being as possessing the status it has, or of failing to do so. We speak of showing respect to those worthy of respect by, say, honouring the honourable, praising the praiseworthy, revering the fearful, worshipping the worshipful, and so on. And we may show contempt for the contemptible, and despise the despicable. To treat a being in such a manner, to treat it as it is, is to treat it appropriately, properly, or *fittingly*, in the manner which befits it.

But we may also act unfittingly: we may treat as higher or lower than is appropriate. We may treat people as higher than they are by flattering, by honouring those unworthy of honour, by showing respect which is not due. We treat people as lower than they are when we fail to show due respect, when we show contempt for those who are not contemptible, or when we refuse praise to the praiseworthy. And—to come to justice—to treat people as lower than they are is (sometimes) to do them an injustice. To do people justice is, by contrast, to treat them fittingly—to treat them as indeed they are. Justice finds its home, then, among the various forms of fitting and unfitting treatment.

The status system and its concepts are widely used. So, too, is the height metaphor to express positions of status and

---

[4] The goal of self-realization seems to suppose that a person's true self is indeed a higher self. If this were not so, and self-realization arguments were based only on the goal of overcoming alienation or estrangement, they would be vulnerable to the objection that, even if a person were to have a base true self, there would be a reason—albeit not a conclusive reason, but still a reason—to realize that baseness, thereby overcoming the alienation. The objection is avoided if self-realization arguments are understood as combining the view that, where possible, we have reason to raise ourselves and others, together with a view of how much raising is possible.

related notions. We speak of higher animals, higher degrees, higher courts, the higher divisions of a league; heaven is on high and hell is the underworld; judges sit above their courts, important people sit on platforms at gatherings, and so on. The height metaphor is not the only one we employ, and the etymology of some of the other concepts of the status system draws attention to other metaphors. Thus 'defile' is derived from making foul or dirty, 'deprave' from making crooked, and 'denigrate' from blackening. Nevertheless, it is the height metaphor which dominates our thinking.[5]

What of the value system? This system is employed by those who claim that the right action on any occasion is that which will bring about the maximum possible value (or expected value). The action required of us is, as Moore put it, the one which 'will produce the greatest possible amount of good in the Universe'.[6] This is, of course, the central idea of utilitarianism. There are many variants of utilitarianism, but in so far as it is a single body of thought, it is so by virtue of the endorsement or adaptation of this core idea: that to act rightly is to maximize the good, to produce as much as possible of that which has value.

Utilitarianism is an attractive theory, and its plausibility derives from the plausibility of this central claim. For how, we might wonder, can we deny that it is the good which we ought to try to produce, or that we ought to try to produce more, rather than less, of that which is good? And once this central claim is accepted the rest of classical utilitarianism seems to follow—easily and irresistibly. Classical utilitarianism is the

---

[5] For discussion of this metaphor, see Barry Schwartz, *Vertical Classification* (Chicago, 1981). Schwartz provides evidence of the astonishingly wide use of this metaphor in different cultures (pp. 40 ff.), although it may not be universal (pp. 109–10). He suggests that the widespread use of this particular metaphor is to be explained by the relationship between parent and child. The parent–child relationship is 'universal, found in all times and places, and characterized by a definite moral as well as physical inequality. . . . the physical difference between parent and child represents a code for social inequality. How this physical contrast becomes a code may be explained in terms of the laws of learning' (p. 100).

[6] G. E. Moore, *Principia Ethica* (Cambridge, 1903), 147.

natural conclusion of this way of thinking, and variants which attempt to resist its conclusions seem botched and *ad hoc*. Indeed classical utilitarianism can seem little more than a definition of what it is to act rationally. And, though some of the utilitarian's conclusions can seem unpalatable, they will be irresistible if the utilitarian's system of practical reasoning— the value system—is the only account of what it is to act rationally.

It is a feature of both status and value systems that they cannot be applied without the adoption, or presupposition, of a further theory which, though intimately related to the system, is distinct from it. The use of the value system is possible only by those who are willing to make commitments on the question of what has value, just as the use of the status system presupposes a willingness to assign status. Judgements which employ the value system are made out only when a satisfactory theory of value is on hand, just as judgements which employ concepts from the status system presuppose a theory of status. This is not to deny that we often take questions of value and status for granted; we often assume, for example, that happiness is valuable, or that all people are fundamentally equal in status.

It is important not to confuse value and status. Some terms—general terms like 'good' and 'bad', 'better' and 'worse'—can be used when speaking of both value and status. And it is possible, and even appropriate, to believe that status is sometimes a function of usefulness, or the capacity to produce happiness, which may have value. Typically, man-made objects which have been made with the intention of being used may have their merits judged in accordance with their usefulness. This is hardly surprising since what we make to use is (normally) intended to be useful. But it does not follow from the fact that some object has a particular status because it has value that 'status' and 'value' are synonymous. The status of people, animals, works of art, need not be determined solely—if at all—by their respective capacities to bring about that which is supposed to have value, and certainly we usually suppose that there are other status-conferring attributes besides usefulness, or the capacity to bring about whatever we believe has intrinsic value.

The value and status systems present a number of contrasts. Firstly, although both systems combine simplicity and complexity, they are simple and complex in different ways. Utilitarianism is a consequentialist theory of supposedly universal application, and this brings complexity. The utilitarian must try to work out what the future holds, and must, ideally, try to assess all the possible consequences of all available actions. Utilitarians must come to terms with the natural and social sciences, with game theory and risk analysis, and so on. Determining how one should act is, on the utilitarian account, a task of great complexity. But simplicity is also a striking feature of utilitarianism, and of the system of practical reasoning—the value system—which utilitarianism embodies. The complexity lies only in operating the system, not in understanding it. As far as concepts are concerned, the utilitarian travels light, distinguishing between value and disvalue (positive and negative utility), between means and ends. But it is difficult to imagine a simpler—some may say elegant, others impoverished—system of practical reasoning.

Utilitarianism's elegant simplicity and conceptual economy is achieved by an eschewal of classification. By contrast, using the status system typically involves employing schemes of classification, often of some complexity. Theories of status are theories of classification, and the status system includes many concepts which are themselves to be made sense of in terms of classifying and misclassifying. The array of concepts found within the status system can make reasoning in this system seem chaotic and reliant on intuition. A drive for order within the status system can lead to the view that there is a single (and complete) hierarchy or scale—as in the idea of the great chain of being (and the principle of plenitude). But use of the concepts of the status system does not imply a belief in any *particular* hierarchy. The system of concepts may be employed—and, of course, usually is employed—in connection with an array of different scales, with different parameters, different virtues, different status-affecting attributes, and with particular entities and beings able to occupy different places in different scales. Our using the status system requires only that we agree that it makes sense to talk of (different) levels.[7]

The simplicity of the status system—in theory at least—comes in its operation. There is no algorithm calling for complex calculations to determine right actions; rather the requirement that degradation and unfitting treatment be avoided provide comparatively simple constraints on permissible courses of action.

A second contrast between the two systems appears if we compare the use of quantification. Utilitarianism, which employs the value system, emphasizes quantification. Quantification is essential if there is to be maximization. Whether the quantification can be achieved is, of course, an open question. The status system has no comparable drive towards quantification. This is not to deny that certain forms of treatment may involve quantification—as in, say, the giving of three cheers, or a twenty-one-gun salute. But, though the ordinality of such quantities often corresponds with the relative status being marked, the cardinality seems often to be arbitrary. Even here, then, where quantification may make a brief foray into the status system, it is generally quantification only of a relatively superficial kind.

Thirdly, the two systems embody very different views of the relationship between required action and existence. When we employ the value system we suppose that there is reason to act to change, or to prevent changes, if, in so doing, we can create what has positive value or destroy what has negative value. We are invited to view our actions as *creative* or

---

[7] The complexity of the status system is reflected in the way most of us conduct much of our practical reasoning. Rarely do we reason only in terms of value and disvalue, of efficiency and expected utility; rather we make use of the concepts of the status system—respect and contempt, virtues and vices, dignity and degradation, justice and honour, and so on. It is the concepts of this system which litter works of literature, and through which conflicts, dilemmas, and tragedies are explored. One might even hazard that it is the complexity of the status system—the plethora of hierarchies, the numerous diverging arguments—which make a rich literature possible.

destructive, as preserving or preventing. As we saw, we are, according to Moore, to produce the greatest possible amount of good in the universe. At the heart of utilitarianism is the idea that the point of action is to create, to bring into existence, what has value.[8] When we turn to the status system, the focus on creating and destroying falls away. Instead action is viewed as treating (of treating fittingly or mistreating), or as elevating or lowering what already exists or will exist. We are to raise those beings which do or will exist as far as their nature, their potential, allows. We should encourage people to live lives which are noble, virtuous, and civilized; we should try to prevent, where not inappropriate, those who will live from being contemptible, unworthy, uncivilized, depraved, and brutish. But it is not to be supposed that we have reason to try to 'maximize status' by, say, trying to turn as much base matter into as many noble human beings as quickly as possible. There is no requirement to act so as to create noble beings *per se*.

There is, then, reason to reject the view that the value system is simply a spelling out of the requirements of rationality, that it is the only system of practical reasoning, for we need not view our actions exclusively as productive or destructive, or as acts of prevention or preservation. To be sure, some actions are to be viewed in this way. But to insist on viewing all actions as, first and foremost, either creative or destructive is to distort: the point of kissing, or removing one's hat or shoes when entering a holy place, will hardly be understood if such acts are interpreted as attempts to produce something. (Such actions may, of course, have effects.) The relevant notions to interpret such actions are not creating and destroying, but treating and expressing.

---

[8] This is, perhaps, a concern particularly appropriate for people who consider themselves able and even duty-bound to play a role which others might reserve for a god: man is viewed as a producer, a creator. Historically, of course, utilitarianism has usually been associated with a humanistic conception of value (happiness, welfare, pleasure, preference satisfaction). But even in its conception of action utilitarianism is humanistic, for in insisting that our fundamental responsibility is to create, utilitarianism discourages any belief that the ultimate purposes of gods and mankind might be different.

Utilitarianism views action in a particular way; it uses a mould which will distort if it is applied without restriction. The utilitarian approach also invites distortion when considering reasons for action. Here the tendency is to assume that the only reason to act is to create, destroy, and so on. The view that we should seek to produce is associated with a particular class in a particular type of society. But it is not an obvious truth that this is the sole point of life, or the point of all action.

Given these striking contrasts it is plausible to view the two systems as distinct. Each system has not only its own distinctive patterns of argument and reasons for action; when we move from one system to the other even the manner in which action itself is to be viewed seems to change: one system is concerned with what ought to exist, the other with how we ought to act with regard to what is taken to have the question of its existence already settled. Given this fundamental distinction it is hard to see how one system could be reduced to the other without distortion.[9]

---

[9] The irreducibility of these systems seems to be one of a number of parallels between the status and value systems, on the one hand, and the Aristotelian and Newtonian systems for explaining why bodies move, on the other. According to the Aristotelian account, bodies tend to move towards the proper place of their kind—earth's place being the lowest, then water, air, and fire. Thus earth and water tend to fall, air and fire to rise. The Aristotelian account's explanation employs the notion of a proper or natural place. Like the status system, this account relies heavily on qualitative distinctions, and finds little place for quantification. The Newtonian explanation is based on the mutual attractive forces of gravitational masses. This account eschews qualitative distinctions as far as possible, and avoids talk of proper or natural places; like utilitarianism it is quantitative, its fundamental assumptions startlingly simple and elegant. The Aristotelian and Newtonian systems appear radically distinct, and from them flow radically distinct types of explanation for the movement of bodies; and because the systems of ideas are so distinct we should not be surprised if the explanations are irreducible. And just as there are radically distinct systems of ideas by which we may explain why bodies move, so, it seems, there are radically distinct systems of ideas by which we may explain how people should act.

1.3 Justice as a Status System Concept

We have located the notion of justice in our moral thinking, by placing it in a particular system of ideas—the status system. But what are the implications of viewing justice as a concept of the status system? Viewing justice in this way will affect how we answer three questions. Firstly, it will affect what we view as the primary domain of justice. We apply the notion of justice to agents, actions, and states of affairs. We speak of people, what they do, and outcomes (the consequences of actions and failures to act) as being just and unjust. It is plausible to suppose that any account of justice will view one of these applications as prior, requiring that applications to the other domains be understood by reference to the use of justice in the primary domain. To accept that justice is to be located in the status system, to accept justice as fittingness, is to view actions as primary as far as justice is concerned. Justice is to be understood as treating fittingly, and we treat by acting (or failing to act). A just person is then to be understood as someone who has a disposition to act justly, and an unjust state of affairs as one which comes about through an unjust act or omission.

Secondly, viewing justice as a status system concept will affect our view of why we should act justly. It will affect our view of what reasons for action we act contrary to when we act unjustly. As we have seen, we distinguish between the raising or lowering of beings or entities, and the treating of beings or entities as if they have a status other than that which in fact they have. Thus there is a distinction between degrading actions which make, or tend to make, less (acts which make someone less than human, make someone unreliable, acts of desecration, and so on), and unfitting actions which *treat* as less (acts which treat someone as less than human, treat someone as unreliable, acts of irreverence, and so on). This distinction reflects a distinction between two types of reason for action we usually suppose we have, and which the status system accommodates: the reason we have not to degrade, or to prevent elevation; and the reason we have not to act in ways which treat beings and entities unfittingly, as having a status other than that which they have. To accept that justice is a status concept is, then, to accept that the reason for action which we act contrary to when we act unjustly is the reason we have to treat beings as having the status they have. This is why, if we accept justice as fittingness, we should act justly.

I shall not claim that we do indeed have such a reason to act, only that if we do not have such a reason then we have no reason for acting justly *per se*. I do not want to claim that this reason for action is necessarily primitive, in the sense that no reason can be given why we ought to treat beings and entities as having the status they have. Certainly it seems that such a reason for action is distinct from any reason we have to maximize that which has value. But I do not want to exclude other possibilities, for example the claim that our duty to act justly rests ultimately on our duty not to degrade. But I shall not pursue that possibility.

Finally, I want to note the implications of viewing justice as a status concept for the question of what is presupposed by any substantive view of what is just and what unjust. What is it that people who disagree on substantive questions of justice are disagreeing about? How do substantive disagreements arise? If we accept justice as fittingness then there are two principal sources of disagreement.

Firstly, there can be disagreements over which attributes are status-affecting. If we disagree over whether an attribute affects the status of its bearer, then we will disagree over what treatment is unjust. Employing the status system presupposes that we take a view on what confers status, and disagreements over how attributes affect status will feed through into disagreements over what justice requires.

Secondly, disagreements on substantive questions of justice may arise from disagreements over what constitutes treating someone as the bearer of a particular attribute. If you believe that a particular action constitutes treating as untrustworthy, say, and I do not, then we may disagree about the justice of such an action, whilst agreeing that trustworthiness is a virtue (and about who possesses that virtue). Such a dispute will concern the interpretation of action, that is, the attaching of meaning to action. What is at issue is the meaning of the action. This meaning need not coincide with what an observer of the action happens to infer from the action, nor with the actual beliefs of the actor. The meaning of what we do, like the meaning of what we say, is to be distinguished from what our hearers infer, and from our own beliefs. If I treat you as untrustworthy when you are not, I may do you an injustice even if it is the case that I do not believe you to be untrustworthy. Punishing the innocent is unjust even where those who punish do not believe those they punish to be guilty. If, as seems plausible, we may do an injustice to people merely by thinking them less than they are, then whether we do *that* injustice will, of course, depend on our actual beliefs. The point is not that our actual beliefs are irrelevant to justice, but that the holding of true beliefs is not sufficient to ensure the avoidance of injustice.

The question of the nature of justice, and the question of whether justice is indeed a status system concept, are important questions in their own right. Given the significance we attach to justice we can hardly view its nature as a matter of little intrinsic interest. But as, if sound, these arguments show, how we understand justice affects what we understand disagreements about what is just and what unjust to be disagreements about, and how we should set about resolving those disagreements. We are not, then, concerned only with the account of the nature of justice for its own sake. Viewing justice as a status system concept can be expected to illuminate what is at issue when people disagree about substantive questions of justice.

1.4 *Injustice and Other Forms of Unfitting Treatment*

Although I shall claim that all unjust treatment is unfitting, I shall not claim that all unfitting treatment is unjust. We may distinguish injustice from other forms of unfitting treatment, and certainly the notion of justice, as generally understood, excludes calling certain forms of unfitting actions unjust. How do we do this? How do we distinguish injustice from other forms of unfitting treatment?

We should not expect the boundaries between injustice and its near neighbours—such concepts as disrespect and contempt—to be sharply defined; but there are, I want to suggest, a number of considerations which encourage or discourage calling particular forms of unfitting treatment unjust. Reluctance to call an unfitting action unjust may stem from either or both of two sources: a doubt that the being treated is able to be treated unjustly, and a doubt that the agent acting is able to treat unjustly. The first requirement—that the being treated must be able to be treated unjustly—raises the question: to whom is justice owed? The second requirement raises the question: who is able to do an injustice? What conditions do we suppose need to be satisfied if someone is to be able to act unjustly, as against with undue contempt, or without due respect? I will look at these questions in turn.

Who or what is able to be treated justly and unjustly? To whom is justice owed? There are some comparatively clear cases: we normally suppose that the treatment of persons can be just or unjust, whereas the unfitting treatment of the natural environment, books, buildings, significant symbols (flags, for example), and sacred places we describe as treatment with contempt, or without due respect. We can treat the planet with contempt, but hardly do it an injustice. The question of whether it is appropriate to refer to the unfitting treatment of animals, especially the higher animals, as unjust is more disputed. *If* we take the view that such treatment is not unjust, what distinction are we marking in our use of respect and contempt, and justice? What is it about a being which, we suppose, makes it able to be treated unjustly, as against merely without due respect?

The distinction we will be drawing here, I want to suggest, is between a being which has the capacity to understand the treatment it receives as fitting or unfitting (or, perhaps, the potential to develop such a capacity), and one which does not.

This capacity, in turn, seems to presuppose that the being treated is one which has, or has the potential to have, a conception of itself and its status, and some capacity to interpret what happens to it as constituting being treated as a being with some particular status.[10] Justice and injustice (together with the capacity to be insulted)—unlike the receipt and denial of respect—we seem to restrict to beings we suppose to have the capacities (or potentiality to develop the capacities) for consciousness, including consciousness of status, and interpretation.[11] If it is indeed these capacities which

[10] It is widely accepted that, at least from some point, it is possible to treat unfittingly and without due respect beings with only the potentiality to develop a consciousness of themselves and a capacity to interpret, but whether *at that same point* such unfitting treatment is to be described as unjust is not a question on which there seems to be general agreement.

[11] Rawls claims that moral persons are the 'sorts of beings' who 'are owed the guarantees of justice', and that moral persons are distinguished by the fact that they are 'capable of having (and are assumed to have) a conception of their good', and 'are capable of having (and are assumed to acquire) a sense of justice' (John Rawls, *A Theory of Justice* (Oxford, 1972) 505). Rawls does not claim that moral personality is necessary in order to be owed justice, only that it is sufficient.

The capacities of consciousness and interpretation seem to lie behind Rawls's conditions. Beings capable of having a conception of their good are said to be owed justice: but such beings must, presumably, be able to conceive of themselves if they are to be able to conceive of a good as their good. And it is plausible to suppose that this (sufficient) condition of Rawls goes beyond what is necessary, for it is not clear why we should deny that a being which is conscious of itself, but which is unable to have a conception of its own good, could not be done an injustice. (It may be that beings capable of having a conception of their good must be free, and thus are able to be done the injustice of being treated as unfree when they are not. And if only beings with such a capacity are free, then only beings with such a capacity are able to be done that injustice. But it does not, of course, follow that they are the only beings able to be done any sort of injustice.) Further, it seems plausible to associate Rawls's second condition—having a sense of justice—with the capacities for consciousness of self and status, and the capacity to interpret. It is difficult to imagine how a being lacking these capacities could have a sense of justice. It is plausible to suppose that the conceptions we have of ourselves are, at least largely, constructed on the basis of our understanding of the manner in which we are treated by others. To that extent to be done an injustice is to have one's conception of one's self and one's status threatened. It is, presumably, this capacity to threaten the self-image of a conscious being which explains why it is such a notable feature of treatment perceived to be unjust that it has the capacity to occasion strong emotional responses, why we feel resentment and indignation when we believe we have been

distinguish beings which we suppose are able to be done an injustice from those which are not, we must be willing to accept that if we came to believe that there are animals which possess these capacities, it would be justice which they are owed. This seems plausible.

This account of the distinction is consistent with the widely held view that beings owed justice (as against mere respect) are superior in status to those who are not. (The claim that those who are owed justice are superior to those who are not is, I take it, common ground between those who would describe the unfitting treatment of animals as unjust and those who would not.) A being which has, or at least is able to have, an awareness of itself, its status, and a capacity to understand that it is being acted towards is generally supposed to have a status superior to one which does not.

Finally, we may note that this condition is plausibly connected with justice, at least if justice is taken to be a member of the fittingness family of concepts. It does not introduce alien concepts to specify an additional condition which unfitting treatment must satisfy if it is to be unjust: the notions of status and treatment are at the very heart of the system within which justice is located. The additional element required for beings to be able to be treated justly or unjustly is simply that they must be able, in some sense, to understand the notions of status and treatment and their application to themselves. The

---

treated unjustly. We resent being treated as if we were less than (we think) we are. We are jealous of our status, and jealous when those whom we do not consider our equals are treated as if they are; and we are envious of those whom we regard as no better than ourselves, but who are treated as if they are.

We cannot argue that animals are not owed justice simply because they cannot give it. It may turn out that what cannot give justice cannot be owed it, but in itself an inability to give justice seems not to exclude a being from being owed justice. To be sure there may be a reason why justice is owed to those who can give justice, which does not apply in the case of those beings who cannot give justice. Such a reason may be grounded on reciprocity: 'Those who can give justice are owed justice. . . . By giving justice to those who can give justice in return, the principle of reciprocity is fulfilled at the highest level' (ibid. 510–11). Those who cannot reciprocate cannot be owed justice *on the basis of reciprocation*. But it does not, of course, follow that those who cannot reciprocate cannot be owed justice.

distinction between those beings of which this is true and those of which it is not seems of such significance that it is hardly surprising that we should wish to mark it in our classification of fitting and unfitting treatment.

I turn now to the question of what conditions need to be satisfied if a being is to be able to act unjustly, as against, say, with undue contempt or without due respect. As before, we should not expect precise conditions. Nevertheless, there are, it seems, occasions on which we tend not to describe an action as unjust, even though it is an unfitting action, and the being treated is a person.

Justice is, as we have seen, closely related to classifying: injustice involves a particular type of misclassification. To treat people unjustly is to act towards them as if they are members of a different status class from that which, in fact, they are. To classify is to judge, to misclassify is to misjudge. Injustice, then, involves misjudgement, and justice is, *par excellence*, the virtue to which those who are specially charged with making judgements are to aspire.

Now we may say of a judgement that it is mistaken, that it is a misjudgement, and on that ground reject it. But we may also question a judgement if we believe that it is beyond the competence of the judger to make the judgement. Competence can most easily be questioned when there is an explicit procedure for appointment to a position of judgement. If the appropriate procedures have not been followed for the appointment of a referee, a Supreme Court judge, an external examiner, and so on, the judgements made can be rejected, not as unjust, but as made without the necessary competence or authority.

We may reject judgements on grounds of competence in less rule-governed circumstances, as when, for example, a person is said to be disqualified from making a judgement on grounds of ignorance, particularly ignorance of a thorough going nature. If I claim that Smith is a more eminent scholar in the field of classical philosophy than Brown, but I do not read Greek, and my knowledge of the area is only of the most fleeting kind, you might describe my judgement as unjust.

But this would be generous—it would be to treat my judgement with a respect it did not deserve. A better criticism would be to say that I did not know what I was talking about, that I lacked the competence to make judgements in these matters.

Questions of competence have a certain priority over questions of judgement. If you successfully challenge my competence to judge (in a given context), this places under a cloud all my judgements (in that context). You do not need to go on and assess the judgements made, although you may elect to do so. You may say that I was not competent to judge a book prize but that, as it happened, I managed to avoid making a complete hash of it.

Now I want to suggest that where an unfitting action gives expression to a judgement which, for some reason, the actor is supposed to lack the competence or authority to make, we tend not to call the unfitting action unjust. Justice and injustice are very much the province of those who do not lack (or are supposed not to lack) any necessary competence to judge. Contempt and disrespect (and insults) have no such presumption.

Consider some cases of unfitting treatment which it may seem inappropriate to call unjust even though the being treated is supposed not to lack consciousness and a capacity to interpret. Contrast the positions of a judge and defendant in a court of law. A judge who treats a petty criminal as evil may be said to act unfittingly and unjustly, whereas the defendant who abuses the judge may be said to act unfittingly but with disrespect rather than unjustly. In accepting that the unfitting actions of the judge may be unjust, but that the unfitting actions of the defendant may not, we seem, implicitly, to be accepting that the judge does not lack any authority to judge, but that the defendant does.

The relationship between the player of a game and a referee or umpire is similar. The referee is required to make decisions, and if they are the wrong decisions they may be unjust. But when a player abuses a referee, the referee, although treated unfittingly, is said to be treated with contempt and without respect, rather than unjustly. Here again this is tantamount to accepting that the referee has authority to judge, and that the player does not.

The lawcourt judge and the football referee are cases where the competence to judge is normally taken as given unless denied. To call the decisions of the judge or referee unjust, therefore, is, implicitly, to accept, because it is to leave unchallenged, the judge's or referee's competence. If the context is such that lack of competence is taken as given (unless challenged), the use of 'just' and 'unjust' denies that denial, implying that those who are passing judgement are indeed competent. A player who abuses a referee *may* be described as treating the referee unjustly, but this would be to make a point, not about the player's treatment of the referee *qua* referee, but about the person holding the office of referee. In other words, it would be to make a point to be taken in a context wider than that within which the authority of the referee and the lack of authority of the player are to be taken as given. Since we may believe that, in the wider context, the player does not lack any necessary competence to judge the referee, that is, the person who holds the office of referee, the player's action may be described as unjust.

One's unfitting actions may fail to be unjust by virtue of a lack of requisite natural as well as conventional authority. Suppose there is a God who has the characteristics usually attributed by Christians. He is, let us suppose, worthy of our trust if anyone is. If I do not trust a friend who is trustworthy I do an injustice. Do I do God an injustice if I do not trust him? There is, at least, a tendency not to describe such an action in these terms. Lack of faith in God may be impious and constitute failing to show proper respect and regard. But to say that one has done God an injustice is itself presumptuous; it is to acknowledge an error, but to do so in a way which fails to show due deference.

Our reluctance to call our unfitting treatment of God unjust reflects our presupposition of God's superior status. To call any treatment of God by us unjust is, by implication, to deny that we lack the competence to judge God. But inferior status to the person judged disqualifies one from sitting in judgement—or so it was long thought. Commoners cannot sit in judgement over nobles, subjects over sovereigns, nor mere mortals over God.[12] It is for this reason that to call any treatment of ours towards God unjust would be presumptuous; it would be to pretend to a competence to judge God which (it is normally assumed) we lack. Of course, we no longer hesitate to describe our judgements of our rulers as just and unjust. But that is simply a reflection of the democratic belief that we do not lack any necessary competence to judge our rulers.

These examples suggest, then, that the use of 'unjust' is itself governed by status: that there is a tendency to view injustice as something we can do only to those who are no more than our equals. Sometimes we can lack the status to be able to act unjustly—we can be limited to contempt and disrespect.

Finally, consider the case of paternalistic legislation. One of the criticisms that can be made of inappropriate paternalism is that it is unfitting: it is to treat adults as children and this, for many, is to treat adults as less than they are, as lacking a status-enhancing attribute (say, the capacity to judge where their own interests lie) which is, supposedly, not lacked. This point is made by saying that paternalistic legislation is insulting. There is, however, a tendency not to call such legislation unjust. Why should this be? Of course, those who reject paternalism may deny that the paternalist (the legislator) has a superior status. But to call an action unjust is not to imply that the person treating has a superior status to the person treated: equals can treat each other unjustly.

---

[12] Cf.:

BISHOP OF CARLISLE. Would God that any in this noble presence
Were enough noble to be upright judge
Of noble Richard! then, true noblesse would
Learn him forbearance from so foul a wrong.
What subject can give sentence on his King?
And who sits here that is not Richard's subject?

(Shakespeare, *Richard II*, IV, i. 117–22)

One reason not to call paternalism unjust is that to do so would be tantamount to accepting, by default, the competence of those who treat us paternalistically to judge us. It is true, as just noted, that our equals can do us an injustice. But the context is important here: paternalistic treatment involves one person (or group or body) treating another as inferior. To call that treatment unjust is to allow that claimed superiority to go unchallenged. Those treated with paternalism are wiser, therefore, to express their complaint of unfitting treatment in terms of insults; they may thereby assert that they have been treated as less than they are, but without allowing (even implicitly) the superiority which the paternalistic treatment has also implied. Criticizing paternalism as insulting rather than unjust, then, may be a shrewd move.

I have argued that for an unfitting action to be unjust it must satisfy two conditions. Firstly, it must be an action which involves the treatment of a being to whom justice is owed, a being who can be done an injustice; and secondly, it must be an action done by someone able to do an injustice. To call an unfitting action unjust is to suggest that the treater does not lack any requisite competence to judge the being treated, and that the being treated has the capacity (or potentiality) for consciousness of self and status, and for interpretation. If these conditions are not satisfied, we tend to speak only of a showing of undue contempt or a failure to show due respect. It is worth noting that both these criteria involve the notion of status. To act unjustly one needs a certain status, a certain authority, and if we are to be done an injustice, we need the status of a being to whom justice is owed.

Are these two conditions sufficient for unfitting treatment to constitute injustice or are there other conditions which, if not satisfied, tend to lead us not to call the treatment unjust? I want to consider three other conditions which might be thought necessary: that the person treated must be someone other than the treater; that injustice occurs only when people are treated as *less* (as against more) than they are; and that there is injustice only when the person treated unjustly suffers.

Firstly, consider the claim that justice occurs only when one person is treated unfittingly *by another*. Now it is no doubt true that when we are concerned with justice we are usually concerned with the treatment of one person by another. But it seems mistaken to regard this as an essential feature of justice, to say that injustice is possible only on account of our plurality.[13] We can—and do—say of people that they have done themselves an injustice. Such cases may not constitute the bulk of injustice.[14] They may not rank as particular signifi-

[13] This view is not only very widely held, it is also very confidently held. For example: '. . . "justice" I have no idea how to define, except that its sphere is that of actions which relate to someone else' (G. E. M. Anscombe, 'Modern Moral Philosophy', *Philosophy*, 33 (1958), 4); and 'Justice is a concept which . . . makes no sense if applied to somebody considered completely in isolation from everybody else. . . . This point . . . is really quite obvious' (R. E. Ewin, *Co-operation and Human Values* (Brighton, 1981), 72). The view is attributed to Rawls by Sandel: 'For Rawls, the first feature of any creature capable of justice is that it be plural in number. Justice could not apply in a world where only one subject existed.' (Michael J. Sandel, *Liberalism and the Limits of Justice* (Cambridge, 1982), 50).
      The belief that justice presupposes plurality may encourage, or be encouraged, by another view which is also widely held: the belief that justice is *essentially* concerned with distribution. (Cf.: 'the most valuable general definition of justice is that which brings out its distributive character most plainly: justice is *suum cuique*, to each his due' (David Miller, *Social Justice* (Oxford, 1976), 20). See also Ewin, *Co-operation and Human Values*, 72.) Certainly the notion of distributing seems to come very close to presupposing plurality, if it does not actually do so. The view that justice is essentially distributive is also to be rejected. Needless to say, this is in no way to deny that distributing is very much something which may be done justly or unjustly.
      The tendency to believe that justice is essentially distributive may have been encouraged by the dominance of utilitarianism. Utilitarianism may seem inadequate for lacking a concern for how the good is distributed, and we may think that justice is what utilitarianism overlooks. It is then but a short step to supposing that justice must be essentially concerned with distribution. To think of justice as essentially distributive may be to preserve fundamentally utilitarian ways of thinking, but to tack on a concern for justice.
[14] Although Rawls might be read as suggesting that for Kant all injustice is, or at least includes, an injustice to the self (at least if in acting as if we belong to a lower order we treat ourselves as if we were a member of that lower order): 'Kant speaks of the failure to act on the moral law as giving rise to shame and not to feelings of guilt. And this is appropriate, since for him acting unjustly is acting in a manner that fails to express our nature as a free and equal rational being. Such actions therefore strike at our self-respect, our sense of our own worth, and the experience of this loss is

cant cases of injustice. Nevertheless, for understanding the
nature of justice their existence may be worthy of note. An
account of the nature of justice will be better if it leaves room
for the possibility of injustice to the self.[15] Justice as fittingness accommodates injustice to the self: we do ourselves an
injustice when we treat ourselves as less than we are.

Secondly, consider the claim that we may act unjustly only
if our unfitting action treats someone as less than he or she is.
Can unfitting treatment be unjust if it only treats people as
higher than they are? There seems little doubt that at least
some cases of inappropriately treating as higher offend
against many people's sense of justice. To many it is unjust to
reward people for what they have not done, or to honour
those who are unworthy of honour, or to declare a wrongdoer
innocent. Certainly miscarriages of justice are said to occur
not only when the innocent are convicted but when wrongdoers are acquitted.

It may be argued that these are indeed cases of injustice but
only because if one is inappropriately treated as higher, there
is always another who is inappropriately treated as lower; and
that to treat everyone as more than they are would not be,
ipso facto, unjust. But it seems very doubtful that the offence
to our sense of justice which is given by at least some instances
of people being treated as higher than they are is entirely to be
accounted for in this way.

There is, to be sure, a reluctance to view cases of unfitting
treatment where no one is treated as less than he or she is as
central cases of injustice, for these are cases where no one is
done an injustice. (It is implausible to claim that people who
are treated as more than they are—the unworthy who are
honoured, or the wrongdoers who are declared innocent—are

shame. We have acted as if we belonged to a lower order, as though we were
a creature whose first principles are decided by natural contingencies'
(Rawls, *A Theory of Justice*, 256).

[15] Of course it may be argued that such cases are not really cases of injustice, and that talk of justice here is mere metaphor. But an account of a concept which does not require such a move is always preferable, other things
being equal, to one which does.

done an injustice.) And we may be reluctant to accept that there can be injustice where there is no one who is done an injustice. (After all, the explanation many of us would give for the importance of justice makes reference to the fact that when there is an injustice someone is wronged.) Nevertheless, it seems that we do accept that there can be cases of injustice where no one is wronged; and that we may act unjustly simply by treating people as more than they are.[16] Once again, although these cases may be less important for practical purposes, they are worth noting if our concern is to understand the nature of justice, for any satisfactory account of justice should allow us to understand why our sense of justice can be offended in circumstances where there is no one who is done an injustice.[17] We should reject, then, the view that unfitting treatment of people is unjust only if they are treated as less than they are.

Finally, I want to consider whether suffering (aside from denigration) is required for injustice. Again it is certainly the case that injustice is usually associated with such suffering, and a person who is done an injustice normally suffers as a consequence. Nevertheless, it would be a mistake to say that for an unfitting action to be unjust it must result in suffering by the unfittingly treated person. It is true that treating as higher is usually associated with the receipt of relative benefits or the avoidance of relative suffering—the privileges of

[16] Cf.: 'one can act unjustly without doing anyone an injustice' (Phillip Montague, 'Comparative and Non-comparative Justice', *Philosophical Quarterly*, 30 (1980), 140).

[17] However, one area in which there may be significant injustice without anyone being done an injustice is in the choice of environmental policies and their effect on future generations. If we accept that significantly different policies will lead to different people being born in the future, we may wonder how we are to explain the apparent intergenerational injustice of cavalier policies. If no one who will ever exist is made worse off than they would otherwise be by the adoption of a policy of cavalier use, if there is never anyone who is wronged, wherein lies any injustice? One response to this problem may be to argue that such policies are unjust, albeit not to anyone, because those who adopt them treat *themselves* as more than they are, as having a significance and importance which they simply do not have. (On the non-identity problem, see Derek Parfit, *Reasons and Persons* (Oxford, 1984), esp. ch. 16.)

rank, as we say; and the standard cases of injustice are cases where people are treated as less than they are, and suffer as a result, such suffering being in addition to the denigration. But this need not always be so. To convict people of crimes they have not committed is unjust, even if they are then shown mercy and do not suffer. Indeed being treated as of higher status may bring less welcome treatment; it is possible for the infliction of suffering or denial of benefits to be the mode by which one person is treated as higher than another. And where this is so being done an injustice may be in a person's interests. Suppose, for example, that a rowing team has a tradition of throwing its best rower in the river at the end of each racing season, that Anne is the best rower, but Barbara is thrown in instead. (Suppose also that this practice is not itself unjust.) Anne's treatment is unfitting and unjust—even though she may be delighted to have been done this injustice.[18] She may be happy to forgo the public honour to avoid the unpleasant experience involved. But that is simply to say that being done an injustice sometimes brings benefits. We should not assume, then, that people are done an injustice by being treated unfittingly only if they suffer as a consequence.[19]

I conclude, then, that these three additional putative requirements for injustice are not necessary. This does not, of course, show that the two conditions we identified earlier are

[18] Barbara's treatment is also unjust. In her case there is an institutional injustice: she was entitled not to be thrown in, and was not treated in accordance with her entitlement.

[19] Nor is suffering as a consequence of being treated unfittingly (even by someone not lacking any necessary authority) a sufficient condition of having been done an injustice. People may be treated as higher than they are, and suffer as a result, without having been done an injustice. Students who are given higher grades than they deserve for a particular course, and as a result are excluded from consideration for a career they wish to pursue on grounds of over-qualification, may have some reason to complain for having been awarded higher grades than deserved; but it would be odd to claim that such students have been done an injustice by the award, irrespective of the consequences. The inappropriate award of such grades is, rather, one of those cases of injustice where there is no one who has been done a (non-comparative) injustice. A mere coincidence of unfitting treatment and suffering is not, then, sufficient for someone to have been done an injustice.

sufficient, but it may provide some reason for thinking that they may be.

1.5 Comparative Justice and Equality

I began this chapter with the example of treating a trustworthy person as untrustworthy, an example which, I claimed, manifested the form of all injustice. In that case the injustice was non-comparative. I want to end by considering some cases of comparative injustice. Comparative justice, I believe, fits relatively easily into the schema which justice as fittingness offers, and my discussion of such injustice will therefore be brief. But I begin with the distinction between comparative and non-comparative justice itself.[20]

When we employ the notion of justice we are often concerned with comparing one person with another, and one person's treatment with another's. This is particularly so when we wish to assess whether some distribution of benefits and burdens is fair. Though such comparisons are often needed to determine what justice requires, it is not true that judgements of justice always involve comparisons between people and the respective treatment they receive. The punishment of an innocent person is unjust, and this is so irrespective of that person's relative standing, and of how others are treated.[21]

Whereas treating people as less (or more) than they are *simpliciter* is non-comparatively unjust, treating people as less (or more) than they are, relative to another or others, is comparatively unjust. If Adam and Barry are both trustworthy, then to praise the trustworthiness of Adam but to refuse similarly to praise Barry is to treat Barry unjustly, not only non-

[20] See Feinberg, 'Noncomparative Justice', 265–306. Feinberg's account of the distinction is discussed in Montague, 'Comparative and Non-comparative Justice', 131–40; and in Joshua Hoffman, 'A New Theory of Comparative and Noncomparative Justice', *Philosophical Studies*, 70 (1993), 165–83.

[21] Any injustice of age discrimination *per se* is likely to be a non-comparative injustice: there may be no comparative injustice if, say, we are all treated (in our turn) as redundant when we are old.

comparatively, but also comparatively, if it is to treat him as comparatively lower when he is not. Similarly, if Adam and Barry are equally untrustworthy, then (undeservedly) to praise Adam as trustworthy but refuse similar praise to Barry would be to treat Barry as comparatively lower when he is not. For that reason it may be described as unjust to Barry, even though non-comparatively he is treated as he deserves. And if Adam is trustworthy and Barry is not, then to praise both for their trustworthiness is to treat Adam as no more worthy of praise than Barry, when in fact he is. Again this may be described as treating Adam unjustly even though he is treated as he is from a non-comparative perspective: he is treated as if he were not comparatively higher, when in fact he is. The basic principle of comparative justice, then, is that comparative treatment should reflect comparative status: people are done a comparative injustice if they are treated as if their status, relative to others, is lower than in fact it is.

A consequence of this basic principle is that, as the familiar dictum says, equals should be treated as equals, and unequals as unequals. Following this dictum is necessary to avoid doing a comparative injustice, but it is not sufficient. We may do a comparative injustice to unequals without treating them as equals. One way, of course, is to treat the inferior as superior to the superior, or the superior as inferior to the inferior. Another is to treat in a way which fails to accord with the degree of difference. (If two students whose work should actually receive 60 and 40 respectively are given grades of 76 and 74 then the student who receives 76 might be said to have been unjustly treated on the ground that that student's true degree of superiority has been denied.)

Although claims of comparative injustice need not rely on the notion of equality or inequality of status (that is, need not be cases of, allegedly, unequals being treated as equals, or equals as unequals), they usually do. This may, in part, be due to there being (now) wide acceptance of the view that all persons have a fundamental equality of status. But another reason is that comparative injustices which do not rely on (or do not rely merely on) equality are much harder to establish than those which do (unless they are cases of superiors being treated as inferior to inferiors, or inferiors as superior to superiors—cases we might reasonably expect to be comparatively rare). In cases other than these an allegation of comparative injustice will rely on a claim that proportionality between comparative status and comparative treatment has not been satisfied. But it is notoriously difficult to establish what proportionality requires. Justice may require that the more serious the crime, the more serious the sentence; but establishing what particular difference in sentence justice requires for crimes differing in some particular degree of seriousness (even leaving aside the question of how degree of seriousness is to be determined) is challenging indeed.

What does treating as equal or unequal require? It is tempting to say that to treat as equal it is necessary to treat in the same way, and to treat as unequal it is necessary to treat in a different way; but it seems that this is not so. Treating all as equals need not require that all be treated the same, for we may treat cases differently without treating them as different. To illustrate: suppose that no human being deserves to be saved, but God chooses (arbitrarily) to save some but not all.[22] No one is done a non-comparative injustice since no one deserves to be saved. But is this still unjust because it is comparatively unjust? Would it be better, as far as justice is concerned, if none were saved rather than only some? We may reject this conclusion if we are willing to argue that although God is treating like cases differently, he is not treating them *as different*. Similarly we may treat cases in the same way without necessarily treating them *as the same*. This time suppose that only some human beings deserve to be saved, but God, being merciful, saves all. Again, if we wish to argue that this is not (comparatively) unjust, we must argue that although God treats all cases in the same way, he does not thereby treat them as the same, as equal. To be sure, treating differently is consistent with treating as different, and treating in the same way is consistent with treating as the same. Thus if we wish to

---

[22] I have taken this example from Feinberg, *Rights, Justice, and the Bounds of Liberty*, 281–2.

avoid even the suspicion of injustice, we will wish to treat equals alike, and unequals differently. Nevertheless, there is a distinction between treating as an equal (or unequal) and treating the same (or differently), and the latter need not be necessary for the former.

Justice requires that we avoid treating equals as unequals, and a number of precepts may be understood as deriving from this general principle. Consider first the principle of reciprocity. It is plausible to suppose that by accepting assistance from someone we acquire an obligation to assist that person in the future should an appropriate occasion arise. If this is indeed a requirement of justice, it is plausible to suppose that it is so because to fail to reciprocate is to treat oneself as superior to one's benefactor. If I really am superior to you, if my interests are more important than yours, then the mere fact that you have helped me on a previous and similar occasion need not be thought to provide a reason why I should assist you. Lack of equality undermines the symmetry to which the idea of reciprocity appeals. If you are indeed my equal, then a failure to reciprocate your assistance at the appropriate time will be to fail to treat you as the equal you are, and thus do you a (comparative) injustice.

A similar argument supports the principle of fairness. According to this principle, if we accept benefits from a basically just system, then we incur an obligation to do our part to maintain that system.[23] In so far as it is unjust to accept benefits from an arrangement while refusing to do one's part to sustain the continued production of those benefits, this is because in so acting we act parasitically, treating ourselves as special, and our interests as more important than those of others.[24] It may be argued, then, that violating the

[23] Cf.: 'when a number of persons conduct any joint enterprise according to rules and thus restrict their liberty, those who have submitted to these restrictions when required have a right to a similar submission from those who have benefited by their submission' (H. L. A. Hart, 'Are there Any Natural Rights?', in Anthony Quinton (ed.), *Political Philosophy* (Oxford, 1967), 61). See also Rawls, *A Theory of Justice*, sects. 18 and 52.

[24] Cf.: 'We are not to gain from the cooperative efforts of others without doing our fair share' (Rawls, *A Theory of Justice*, 343).

principle of fairness is unjust for it is to fail to treat others as our equals.

It seems, then, that if such principles as reciprocity and fairness are requirements of justice, they are so because following them is necessary if we are to treat others as the equals they are supposed to be. Much less plausibly it might be argued that treating equals as equals requires the adoption of the principle of utility. The argument here is that treating all as equal requires giving equal consideration to each person's interests, which in turn requires adopting the principle of utility. But this is a very doubtful argument: to distribute all resources by a lottery in which all have an equal chance does not, on the face of it, fail to treat all as equals. It is not to treat any as having a superior status. But if that is so, then the adoption of utilitarianism cannot be necessary for treating all as equals.

A more plausible view is that adopting utilitarianism is sufficient to treat all as equals (while being necessary to avoid inefficiency). The argument is that utilitarianism, because it singles out no one's interests as being of more intrinsic importance than anyone else's, does not treat anyone as having a superior status to anyone else.[25] If we follow utilitarianism, then, we will treat no one as superior to anyone else; thus adopting utilitarianism is sufficient to ensure the treatment of all as equals.

If adopting utilitarianism is indeed sufficient to treat all as equals, then utilitarianism can be successfully defended against the charge that it may lead to injustice—in so far as injustice is supposed to arise from a failure to treat all as equals. Conversely, if we accept that utilitarianism is sufficient to treat all as equals, but still wish to argue that utilitarianism is consistent with injustice, we must show that in some other way utilitarianism treats people as less than they are. It will not be our equality which utilitarianism fails to respect, but some determinant of our non-comparative status. That is, we

---

[25] Cf. J. S. Mill, *Utilitarianism*, ch. 5, para. 36; (repr. in *Utilitarianism*, ed. Mary Warnock (London, 1962) 319–20).

will need to show how utilitarianism treats us all as less than we are.

Comparative injustices—such as failures to treat equals as equals and unequals as unequals—seem, then, to be readily accommodated by the view that justice is a member of the fittingness family of concepts. Precepts deriving from the principle of treating equals as equals may be viewed as exhibiting, in a transparent manner, the form which, I have claimed, is possessed by all principles of justice. Equality and inequality (in this context) are status concepts. To be an equal is to be of a certain status, albeit one only comparatively specified, and a comparative injustice is done when treatment fails to accord with comparative status. However, as I have noted, justice is not always comparative: injustice does not arise only through failures to treat equals as equals and unequals as unequals. It remains to be seen whether all non-comparative injustice has the form which justice as fittingness requires.

2

Justice and Desert

In the previous chapter I discussed justice at a high level of abstraction, seeking to locate the concept in our practical reasoning, and to distinguish justice from neighbouring concepts. In the present chapter my aim is to make this account less abstract by showing that the language of desert provides an idiom in which to discuss substantive questions of justice. To accept justice as fittingness is to accept that to treat people justly requires no more than that they be treated in accordance with their deserts. So, at least, I shall argue.

The chapter begins with an account of desert itself, and the grounds for viewing the concepts of desert and justice as closely related. I then discuss what is required for treatment to be in accordance with desert. Next I consider some reasons which might be offered for avoiding employing the notion of desert, and argue that such reasons are unpersuasive. Finally, I note the problem cases for the claim that justice requires only treatment according to desert. By implication these are the problem cases for defending justice as fittingness. Thus in identifying these cases the agenda for much of the rest of the book will be set.

2.1 Desert

It is often supposed that justice is simply a matter of getting one's deserts.[1] Whether or not this is an interesting claim

---

[1] For example: 'Justice is getting what one deserves; what could be simpler?' (John Hospers, *Human Conduct: An Introduction to the Problems of Ethics* (New York, 1961), 433); 'it is arguable that justice, in its distinctive

depends on how we understand the concept of desert. If we have a wide notion of desert—if we place few restrictions on its use—any identification of justice with desert will be easy but trivial. I want to argue that justice does indeed require only that all are treated in accordance with desert, *and* that this is so even if desert is narrowly conceived, as indeed it should be. To begin, then, we must consider how the concept of desert is to be drawn.

Desert is a triadic relation, the variables of which are the (putative) deserver, that which is deserved, and the ground or basis of the desert.[2] We may, of course, be content to leave some of the variables implicit—as when we say simply that John is a deserving case—but it is not (conceptually) possible to be deserving of nothing in particular or for no particular reason. Further constraints on the application of desert will stem from constraints on what may satisfy these three variables. What are those constraints?

Firstly, who or what may deserve? Although we are often concerned with personal desert, that is, with cases where the deserver is a person, use of desert is not restricted to such cases.[3] We may say that a poodle, a pig, or a pansy deserves a prize, that flags and holy places deserve respect, that a manuscript deserves to be published, that a railway engine, building, or wilderness deserves to be preserved, and so on. There seem to be no obvious restrictions on what kind of being or thing may be said to deserve. Of course the being or thing has to be deserving (and hence must be of a kind able to deserve)—but this seems to be no more than the requirement that there be a desert basis.

meaning, is to be defined as distribution in proportion to the deserts of possible recipients' (T. D. Campbell, 'Humanity before Justice', *British Journal of Political Science*, 4 (1974), 2); and 'While everyone agrees that justice, almost by definition, is giving people what they deserve, there appears to be little agreement concerning what it is that people deserve' (James P. Sterba, 'Recent Work on Alternative Conceptions of Justice', *American Philosophical Quarterly*, 23 (1986), 1).

[2] My discussion of desert is heavily indebted to Joel Feinberg's 'Justice and Personal Desert', repr. in his *Doing and Deserving: Essays in the Theory of Responsibility* (Princeton, 1970), 55–94.

[3] Cf. ibid. 55.

Secondly, what can be deserved? What is deserved is, usually at least, deserved as a specific form or mode of treatment. Such modes of treating include praising, honouring, criticizing, rewarding, punishing, compensating, grading, and so on. We engage in such practices, thereby treating in particular ways, and such treatment may be deserved or undeserved. Thus what we deserve we may deserve as an honour, grade, reward, punishment, compensation, and so on. Whatever can fulfil such a function can be deserved.

It seems, then, that what is distinctive about desert must in large part derive from the restrictions on what may function as a desert basis. What are those restrictions? Feinberg suggests that in general only facts which are facts about the deserver can function as a basis of desert.[4] Although such a restriction has an intuitive plausibility, it will count for little unless we are able to say what does, and what does not, count as a fact about a deserver. What would a 'fact about' requirement rule out? We might suppose that such a requirement will at least preclude our claiming that, say, students can deserve high grades on the basis that such grades will please their parents.[5] But why should this be so? Why may we not argue that in such a case there *is* a fact about such students to function as a desert basis: why may we not claim that it is a fact about such students that they have parents who will be pleased by their receiving high grades? Perhaps it will be said that such a fact is not a fact about the deserver in the required sense. Perhaps more is required than that there is a fact capable of being expressed in a sentence of which the deserver is the grammatical subject. But if so, what more? And why?[6]

---

[4] 'In general, the facts which constitute the basis of a subject's desert must be facts about that subject' (ibid. 58–9)

[5] The example is Feinberg's: 'If a student deserves a high grade in a course, for example, his desert must be in virtue of some fact about *him*—his earlier performances, say, or his present abilities. Perhaps his teacher *ought* to give him a high grade because it will break his neurotic mother's heart if he does not, but this fact, though it can be a reason for the teacher's action, cannot be the basis of the student's desert' (ibid. 59).

[6] Feinberg allows that: 'The basis of desert may be a complex relational fact, but in that case the subject must be a party to the relation. The basis of desert cannot be wholly separate from the subject' (ibid. 59 n. 6). But it may

38   2. *Justice and Desert*

I shall accept that, in general, desert bases are facts about
the deserver; but I shall not claim that this requirement is a
defining feature of desert and thus able to provide the ultimate
ground of an explanation why some uses of 'desert' are (conceptually) inappropriate. How, then, are we to explain why
having a parent who will be pleased by a high grade cannot
function as a desert basis for such a grade? The explanation is
that a student's status is not affected by whether or not he or
she has such a parent.[7] And what does not affect the status of
the deserver—what does not make the deserver more or less
worthy of respect, admiration, and so on—cannot function as
a basis of desert. So, at least, I want to argue. I shall refer to
this claim as the 'status requirement'.[8]

It is, I suggest, the status requirement which explains why
desert bases are, usually at least, facts about the deserver. We
normally suppose that the status of a being depends on facts
about that being. But if the status of a being depends on facts
about that being, and if desert depends on the status of the
deserver, then desert will depend on facts about the deserver.
Thus the 'fact about' requirement is to be viewed as a consequence of the status requirement, not as, in itself, a defining
feature of desert.

Why should we accept the status requirement, and view it
as a defining feature of desert? Firstly, not only are many
desert bases status-affecting, but their being status-affecting is
something which, normally at least, we expect. Facts which it

be argued that having a parent who will be pleased is not a fact 'wholly separate' from the student in question.

[7] At least we normally assume that this claim may be taken as given. For
those who really do believe that a person's status is (say) enhanced by it
being a fact about that person that he or she has such a parent there may be
no conceptual impropriety in offering such a fact as a basis of desert.

[8] Cf.: 'it is appropriate and correct to say of a subject X, that it deserves
A . . . when X possesses characteristics or has done something B, which constitutes a *positive or negative valuation* of X' (John Kleinig, *Punishment and
Desert* (The Hague, 1973), 62, emphasis added); and 'The range of possible
desert bases coincides with the range of possible bases for *appraising* attitudes' (David Miller, *Social Justice* (Oxford, 1976), 89, emphasis added). By
'appraising attitudes' Miller refers to such attitudes as admiration and
approval (ibid. 88).

is possible to view as status-affecting are readily intelligible as bases of desert: being trustworthy, wise, evil, lazy, strong, eloquent, a vegetarian, old, male, and so on are intelligible as bases of desert to the extent that they may be viewed as grounds for admiration, respect, and so on. (Of course to say that a claim is intelligible is not at all to say that we need accept it.) Where we are at a loss to understand how a given fact—say, that a person was born on a particular day, or has a parent who will be pleased if a high grade has been received—is supposed to be status-affecting we will be at a loss to understand any claim of desert based on that fact.

A further reason to accept the status requirement is that it allows us to make sense of the widely held belief that a lack of responsibility undermines a claim to deserve—the 'desert-responsibility thesis' as I shall call it. I shall examine this thesis in some detail later (7.1–4). Here I want simply to note how widespread acceptance of this thesis supports the view that the status requirement is more than an empirical generalization. Deserts (as against, say, claims of entitlement or need) are often viewed as undermined if we are not responsible for what we do and the characteristics we have. Why should this be so? At least part of the explanation seems to be this: there is an equally wide acceptance of the view that people may not be appraised on the basis of what they are not responsible for (that is, there is no such thing as moral luck). This claim, when combined with the status requirement, implies that desert is undermined by a lack of responsibility. There is nothing comparable to the status requirement in the case of entitlement or need: a denial of responsibility leaves claims based on entitlement and need unaffected. The peculiar vulnerability of desert to a denial of responsibility is based on the status requirement. Conversely, the widespread acceptance of that vulnerability is evidence for the existence of the status requirement.

There are, then, reasons to accept the status requirement. Nevertheless, there are two notable problem cases for the status requirement: desert on the basis of contribution, and desert of compensation. Why are these problem cases?

Consider first the case of contribution. It is often supposed that those who contribute more (to a project, to society, or whatever) deserve to receive more in return.[9] (This is an unobjectionable use of 'desert', or so I shall assume.) Now to be sure some who hold such a view may be willing to base this claim on the further claim that contribution affects status: that the more we contribute the more worthy we are of respect, admiration, and so on. But to many this further claim is implausible. The extent to which people contribute is so often affected by factors outside their control—often a matter of luck or a consequence of the activities of others. Thus many will wish to endorse the view that those who contribute more deserve more but without being committed to holding that contributing (necessarily) affects the status of the contributor. On the face of it, then, deserving on the basis of contribution may be a counter-example to the status requirement.[10]

Compensation is a second case where we may seem to employ desert without any status-affecting basis. It is often held that those who suffer through no fault of their own—and especially those who suffer as a result of another's fault—deserve compensation. (Again the use of 'deserve' here is natural enough.) But it is not generally supposed that our status

[9] Cf.: 'there is no doubt that desert is attributed on the basis of actions, efforts and results produced, and any attempt to say that we are always (confusedly) rewarding and punishing (say) efforts seems to me quite misguided' (Brian Barry, *Political Argument* (London, 1965), 107).

[10] It may also be doubted whether making a contribution is to be regarded as a fact about the contributor. Making a contribution may be no more than something which happens to the contributor; and we do not, normally at least, make inferences about agents (qua agents) merely on the basis of what happens to them. The 'qua agents' is important: we can—and do—make inferences about material objects, say, from what happens to them—that they are impenetrable, have particular densities, and so on. The 'merely' is also important. We might infer from the fact that people are being punished that they had intentionally acted wrongly. (We might be mistaken in making such an inference: by saying that 'we might infer' someone was guilty of intentional wrongdoing I mean no more than that, in some circumstances, we would have a reason for drawing such a conclusion, not that we should have a conclusive reason.) But such an inference cannot be made *merely* from what happens to a person. We must bring in other beliefs, thereby attaching significance to what has happened.

is affected simply because we happen to suffer (through no fault of our own, or through another's fault). The deserving of compensation, then, seems to be a counter-example to the status requirement.[11]

The objection to the status requirement based on compensation may not, at first sight, appear serious, for it may seem that we may argue as follows. People who suffer through no fault of their own deserve compensation simply because they do not deserve to suffer. Thus deserving compensation cannot run counter to the status requirement for, since no positive desert claim is made, no desert basis (status-affecting or otherwise) is presupposed.

But this argument is a *non sequitur*. We may agree that those who suffer through no fault of their own do not deserve to suffer. But to say that someone deserves compensation is to say that that person deserves not to suffer. The argument, then, requires us to move from the claim that a person does not deserve to suffer to the claim that the person deserves not to suffer. But the latter claim does not follow from the former. To say that a person does not deserve to suffer is to say that there is no reason (of a desert-generating type) for that person to suffer. To say that a person deserves not to suffer is to say that there is a reason (of a desert-generating type) for that person not to suffer. And, clearly, it does not follow merely from the fact that there is no reason, of a desert-generating type, for a person to suffer that there is a reason, of a desert-generating

[11] Feinberg appears not to endorse the status requirement—at least in part on the basis of compensation and related notions. He writes: 'It is necessary that a person's desert have a basis and that the basis consist in some fact about himself, but neither of these conditions is sufficient. . . . It is impossible, however, to list the necessary and sufficient conditions for personal desert in the abstract, for the bases of desert vary with the mode of deserved treatment' (Feinberg, *Doing and Deserving*, 61). In his discussion of the various types of deserved treatment he writes that prizes 'are taken to be tangible expressions of admiration' (ibid. 63) and rewards are 'means of expressing recognition, appreciation, or approval of merit or excellence' (ibid. 69). But in his discussion of compensation, reparation, and liability (ibid. 74–6) there is no suggestion that a person deserves compensation on account of a status-affecting desert basis. It would appear, therefore, that Feinberg's view is that desert bases are only sometimes status-affecting, and are not in the cases of compensation, reparation, and liability.

type, for the person not to suffer. Some additional presumption is necessary. Nor can the status requirement be saved by some general presumption that, *ceteris paribus* at least, people who do not deserve to suffer should not suffer. The conclusion we require is not that people should not suffer, but that they *deserve* not to suffer.[12]

Thus the problem for the status requirement remains: we do talk of (some) people who suffer deserving compensation, but we do not suppose that such suffering is status-affecting— that those who suffer in this way become more admirable, more worthy of respect, than they would otherwise have been.[13] Both contribution and compensation pose problems for the claim that the desert basis must always affect the status of the deserver. Nevertheless, the temptation to abandon the status requirement should be resisted. As we have seen,

[12] I will suggest later (2.2) that arguments of this type can be put in an alternative idiom. In that alternative idiom the argument here would go as follows. People who suffer through someone else's fault do not deserve to suffer. Now to fail to compensate is to act as would be appropriate if the person did deserve to suffer. (If we believe people deserve punishment, and they are punished, we believe that compensation for the punishment would be inappropriate.) But to fail to compensate is not in itself to treat a person as deserving to suffer. (In a closely knit family, for example, the actions of one member may cause suffering to another, but to offer compensation may be inappropriate.) A failure to offer compensation, in itself, does not, then, constitute treating as deserving to suffer.

[13] As with contributing, we might doubt that having suffered through no fault of one's own is really a fact about the putative deserver. Again we are concerned here with an event which happens to the deserver, rather than with anything which the deserver does, and on the basis of which inferences about the deserver might be drawn. The unusual character of the desert of compensation has been noted by Kleinig. Kleinig asserts that: 'Desert can be ascribed to something or someone only on the basis of characteristics possessed or things done by that thing or person' (John Kleinig, 'The Concept of Desert', *American Philosophical Quarterly*, 8 (1971), 73) and that: 'If a person deserves compensation for some loss, then he does so not because things will be very difficult for him if he does not get some, but because his loss has been sustained through someone else's mismanagement, negligence or deception, etc.' (ibid.). And at this point Kleinig adds: 'This fits a little awkwardly into the stipulation "characteristics possessed or things done by that thing or person". Perhaps it is closer to the former—damage sustained through no fault of one's own. If no damage is done, no compensation is deserved' (ibid. 73 n. 10). Kleinig is right to think that there is awkwardness here.

the status requirement is more than an empirical generalization, something which merely happens to be true in some
cases. At least normally we *expect* a (putative) desert basis to
be status-affecting. We cannot, of course, ignore the problems
posed for the status requirement by contribution and compensation. But it remains possible that these anomalies are
only apparent. I shall argue later (3.1–3) that this is indeed so.

We have seen, then, that some character is given to desert
by constraints on what may function as a desert basis, and by
the relationship between the desert basis and the deserver. But
further form is provided by constraints on the relationship
between what is deserved and the desert basis. It is to that
relationship that I now turn.

We say (let us suppose) that the most able candidate
deserves the appointment, the better boxer (on the day)
deserves to win the fight. Clearly, the desert basis must be
relevant to what is deserved: the boxer does not deserve the
appointment (coincidences apart), and the most able candidate does not deserve to win a fight. The type of good being
allocated or distributed determines the type of desert basis
which is relevant.[14] Certainly we should not wish to take
irrelevant desert bases into account. But what counts as relevant here? What is it that makes, say, ability a relevant desert
basis so far as appointment is concerned?[15] What is it that
makes being the better boxer (on the day) relevant to deserving to win the fight? Both cases employ the notion of desert;
so a reasonable assumption is that whatever it is that makes
ability to perform a job relevant to deserving an appointment
makes boxing well relevant to deserving to win a fight.

The notion which ties together the desert basis and what is

[14] Cf.: 'in deciding upon the just allocation of a good, it is not necessary
to take account of desert in general, but only of those deserts which are relevant to the good being distributed' (Miller, *Social Justice*, 117–18). See also
William A. Galston, *Justice and the Human Good* (Chicago, 1980), 170.

[15] Of course, we often—though by no means always—have reason to see
the duties of a position are discharged competently, and hence have reason
to appoint someone who is able and likely so to discharge them. But it does
not follow from this that the most (relevantly) able person *deserves* the
appointment.

deserved is *treatment as*. To say that a particular candidate deserves the appointment on the basis of being the most able is (at least) to say that being appointed is a way of being treated as the most able. Similarly, to say that the boxer deserves to win—having fought the better fight—is (at least) to say that winning is a way of being treated as having fought the better fight. If appointment or victory are, respectively, the only ways to be treated as the most able and as having fought the better fight, then denial of appointment or victory will be to treat as not the most able or as not having fought the better fight.

To treat someone as a member of a class X is to act towards that person in such a manner as gives expression to a belief that the person is a member of class X. (The belief need not, of course, be held: we may treat people as guilty, that is, give expression to a belief that they are guilty, without actually believing them to be guilty.[16]) The connection between the desert basis and what is deserved can, then, also be set out in terms of expression. What people deserve is governed by the requirement that they should not be treated in such a manner as gives expression to a false belief about their status-affecting attributes. If the candidate most able to do a job deserves appointment, this is because to fail to appoint that candidate would be to act in such a manner as to give expression to the belief that that candidate is not the most able to do the job. If the better boxer (on the day) deserves to win the fight, this is because in losing he will have been treated in a manner which gives expression to the belief that he was not the better

[16] We may wonder why mere expression should be so significant, particularly since the expression may be of a belief not actually held. One reason may be this: that at least to some degree our identity is constituted by the treatment we receive from (some) others. Just as the meaning of a word can be changed by the practices of native speakers, so, on this view, the practices of those whose actions count can affect who we are. And just as social 'misuse' of language legitimizes itself, so too does social 'mistreatment'. On this view, then, the distinction between the status a person has and the status a person is treated as having is collapsed, and what is wrong with doing an injustice is that it degrades.

fighter.[17] Where failure to give expression to a belief constitutes a tacit denial of that belief then such a failure may constitute a failure to treat in accordance with desert.

In view of the link between desert and expression we
should expect that what is deserved will often be a matter of
convention, for expression is often conventional.[18] To be

[17] In order to have been treated there must be a treater, but in many cases
this requirement is 'satisfied' simply by personification. If I take a substantial risk which just happens to pay off I may claim that I deserve the benefits
I acquire as a reward for my act of bravery. Here the mode of treatment is
rewarding, and nature, fate, or fortune does service as the treater. Similarly,
we suppose that those who play better—show more skill, determination, and
imagination—deserve to win. Of course this does not always happen: sometimes the team which plays better is unlucky and loses. It may be denied its
just reward. Again nature, fate, or fortune does service as the treater, and we
complain that 'there is no justice'. But we do not suppose that there is any
reason to act to produce a just state of affairs. It seems not, then, that we
simply accept that luck is a desirable part of a game and that some lack of
justice is a price we must pay to preserve it. That would not explain why we
consider there is no reason not to attempt to rectify the injustice. Rather, it
seems, our attitude is to be explained by the fact that we do not really believe
that anyone has been treated unjustly—because we do not really believe anyone has been treated. Although we, explicitly or implicitly, personify nature,
fate, or fortune to give some sense to the claim that the victim has been
unjustly treated, for most of us such talk is idiomatic. We do not believe that
there is anyone who has really treated the victim, and we do not, therefore,
believe that anyone has been treated, and hence cannot consistently believe
that anyone has been treated unjustly. It is, then, the absence of a treater
which makes this seem not a genuine case of injustice, and certainly not a
case of injustice calling for prevention or rectification.

[18] Cf.: 'Desert is, in large measure, conventional because it is expressive'
(J. R. Lucas, *On Justice* (Oxford, 1980), 209), and 'To say that the very
physical treatment [of punishment] itself expresses condemnation is to say
simply that certain forms of hard treatment have become the conventional
symbols of public reprobation. This is neither more nor less paradoxical
than to say that certain words have become conventional vehicles in our language for the expression of certain attitudes, or that champagne is the alco-
holic beverage traditionally used in celebration of great events, or that black
is the color of mourning' (Feinberg, *Doing and Deserving*, 100).
   Expression and announcement play a central role in the argument of
Rawls's *A Theory of Justice*. It is claimed to be 'a desirable feature of a conception of justice . . . that it should publicly express men's respect for one
another' (p. 179), and an advantage of the two principles that they 'express
[the notion that men are to be treated as ends and not as means only] visibly
in the basic structure' (p. 180). A publicity condition is imposed on the
choice to be made in the original position (p. 133); and 'Since in justice as
fairness moral conceptions are public, the choice of the two principles is, in

sure, the expression of some beliefs through actions seems natural—as when we hug those we love, and push away those who repel us. But much expression is conventional and artificial. It follows, therefore, that what we deserve is often affected by conventions and rules. Thus it is a mistake to draw too stark a contrast between the naturalness of desert and the conventionality of entitlement (that is, qualification under a rule). Rules and conventions often have a role to play in determining who deserves what,[19] though such rules function at a deeper level than do the rules under which we come to have entitlements. The example of the two rowers discussed earlier (1.4) illustrates how rules and conventions affect desert and entitlement at different levels. Anne's liability to be thrown in the river, and Barbara's entitlement not to be thrown in, follow directly from the rule that the best rower is to be thrown in the river. But the convention also affects, if less directly, how Anne and Barbara are to be treated if they are to be treated in accordance with their deserts, that is, in accordance with their (relevant) status-conferring attributes (in Anne's case being the best rower, in Barbara's case being not the best rower). Anne deserves to be treated as the best rower whatever the prevailing conventions are. But she deserves *to be thrown in the river* only because of the prevailing convention.

With this account of desert on hand we are in a position to explain why desert provides an alternative idiom in which to express justice as fittingness, why there is a congruency between justice as fittingness and the view that desert is central to justice. Firstly, the notion of treating—central to just-

effect, an announcement' (p. 161). These considerations also come into play with the derivation of the natural duties: 'Once we try to picture the life of a society in which no one had the slightest desire to act on these duties, we see that it would express an indifference if not disdain for human beings that would make a sense of our own worth impossible. Once again we should note the great importance of publicity effects' (p. 339). Expression is also central to the 'Kantian interpretation' of justice as fairness, and the arguments which rely on expressing our nature as free and equal rational beings. See pp. 251–7, 476, 515, 561, and 572.

[19] Or, in view of the reductive argument of 5.2, who deserves what, *independent of any entitlement*.

ice understood as a member of the fittingness family of concepts—appears in the analysis of desert. It is the notion of
treating which provides the link between the desert basis and
what is deserved. Secondly, given the status requirement, to
fail to treat people in accordance with their deserts is to fail to
treat them in accordance with the status-affecting facts about
them, that is, fittingly. (And, we might add, any requirement
that the desert basis be a fact about the deserver has its
counterpart in the idiom of fitting treatment: if a desert basis
must be a fact about the deserver, it follows that to fail to treat
people in accordance with their deserts is to fail to treat them
as they are.) Our conclusion, then, is this. If the source of
injustice is always unfitting treatment, then the concept of
desert is well-fashioned to play a central role in determining
what is just; and if we treat people in accordance with their
deserts, we will not act unjustly.

Given the close relationship between justice (conceived as a
member of the fittingness family of concepts) and treating in
accordance with desert, it is not surprising that those uses
of the concept of justice which readily exemplify justice as
fittingness—such as treating in accordance with a non-
comparative false derogatory judgement and failing to treat as
an equal—are cases where the injustice is manifestly a failure
to treat in accordance with desert. If I describe your last philosophical paper as a piece of plagiarism when in fact it was all
your own work, or if I treat you as a being of inferior status
to me when you are not, then I will do you an injustice, and
this is readily expressed using 'desert': you will have deserved
better treatment than you received.

If we treat in accordance with desert, we will not act
unjustly, but, of course, the converse does not hold: we may
fail to treat in accordance with desert but not act unjustly. The
natural environment and animals may deserve to be treated
with respect even if it is not unjust to fail to so treat them. God
may deserve our trust even if we would not act unjustly if we
failed to give it. Neither of the requirements for injustice over
and above unfitting treatment which we noted earlier (1.4)—
that the treater does not lack any requisite competence to

judge the being treated, and that the being treated has the capacity (or potentiality) for consciousness of itself and status, and for interpretation—restrict the use of desert. Thus we may fail to treat in accordance with desert but not act unjustly. Desert, rather than justice, is the wider notion.

2.2 *Treating according to Desert*

If desert is to have any role in determining what is just, then it is important to understand what is required if we are to treat people in accordance with their deserts. People who are deserving (have a particular desert) ought to be treated as deserving (as having that desert) and ought, other things being equal at least, to get what they deserve. To treat the deserving as undeserving is not to treat in accordance with desert. This requirement is relatively straightforward. The more complex issue is whether this is the only requirement. In particular, what are we to say in the case of the undeserving? What, if anything, does treating according to desert require where a person is considered to have no (relevant) deserts?

There are two views to consider. The first is taken by Kleinig, who claims that, if people are undeserving—have no relevant deserts—then nothing follows as to what they should or should not get; and there can be no objection—as far as deserts are concerned—no matter how they are treated.[20] Whatever the undeserving get they are not treated in a way which is contrary to their deserts. This is a plausible view. If no one deserves a share of my estate, then I may, it seems, distribute it how I like without acting contrary to desert. Of course, if there is someone who not merely does not deserve a share, but deserves not to have a share, I would act contrary to desert if I gave a share to that person. Such a person does have a relevant desert. But where there are no deserts at all—including deserts not to receive—I may do what I like and still treat people in accordance with their deserts.

[20] 'From the claim "X does not deserve to get A" nothing strictly follows about what X ought to get' (Kleinig, *Punishment and Desert*, 72).

A different view is offered by Sverdlik, who suggests that we can go wrong in the way we treat people who have no deserts if we treat them as having deserts they do not have.[21] This view is also plausible. Innocent people do not deserve punishment, and to punish them is unjust. If we take this view, then we allow that people who have no (relevant) deserts can be treated unjustly, and not in accordance with desert. They can be wrongly treated by being treated as having deserts they do not have.

The two approaches seem incompatible: if people have no (relevant) deserts, then it either does, or it does not, follow that any treatment of them is in accordance with desert. In practice we tend to adopt both views, but restrict their application. We distinguish between good and ill desert, and we tend to a Kleinigian approach when thinking of deserving well, and a Sverdlikian approach in dealing with deserving ill. We suppose that where, but only where, we are concerned with ill desert people must not be treated as having deserts they do not have.

This may work well enough in practice, most of the time at least. But it is untidy and inelegant, and it is hardly satisfactory from an analytical point of view. Firstly, if the two views are incompatible, it is very doubtful we should derive much reassurance from the fact that we are adept at employing them in distinct areas. That practice may obscure any deeper inconsistency to which we are committed in adopting the different views—but it will not remove it. Secondly, the Kleinigian can point out that if there really are no relevant deserts to consider, there can be no reason (of a kind which generates a desert claim) that can be acted contrary to by any treatment, while the Sverdlikian can argue that there is always something wrong—inappropriate—with treating people as having deserts they do not have. On the face of it these arguments for the different positions can be made irrespective of whether we are dealing with well or ill desert. And thirdly,

---

[21] '. . . the scapegoat has no deserts, and is harmed: this is what is wrong' (Steven Sverdlik, 'The Logic of Desert', *Journal of Value Inquiry*, 17 (1983), 323).

adopting different approaches for well and ill desert provides an opportunity for confusion on occasions where it is unclear which we are dealing with. The case of the rowing team and their custom of throwing their most able rower in the river discussed earlier (1.4, 2.1) is an example of such a case. If Barbara is not the best rower, she does not deserve to be thrown in. Is Barbara treated in accordance with her deserts if she is thrown in? If we think of being thrown in the river as an honour, and thus think we are dealing here with well desert, then, taking a Kleinigian approach, the action is not contrary to desert. Barbara simply receives better than she deserves. But if we think of being thrown in as an unpleasant experience, a case of suffering to be dealt with according to the Sverdlikian approach, then we will conclude Barbara's treatment is contrary to desert. She is treated as having deserts she does not have.

To be assured that we are not committed to any inconsistency we need to be assured that although in our everyday thinking we may endorse both approaches (at different times), we do not need to. We need to be assured that at least one of these approaches will work satisfactorily throughout. (If we were able to show that only one is able to work satisfactorily throughout, we will have good reason to adopt that approach.)

I want to suggest that either approach may be adopted throughout, for each approach, used with care, can accommodate the concern which encourages us sometimes to adopt the other. The point is that if we do adopt one approach throughout, we must take care to avoid a pitfall. The nature of the pitfall we need to ensure we avoid depends on which of the approaches we adopt.

Suppose we take the Sverdlikian view: we must not be treated as having deserts we do not have, and those with no deserts must be treated accordingly. How is this to be reconciled with our view that justice does not require that people should get only the benefits they deserve—our firm conviction that generous and benevolent actions are not contrary to justice? The point here is that such actions are not contrary to desert because in performing such actions we do not treat a person as deserving (what they receive). What we do is something which is related, but which can be distinguished: we give people what we would need to give them in order to treat them as deserving. Although getting such a benefit may be necessary if one is to have been treated as deserving, it may not be sufficient.[22]

What of the alternative approach? Here we are treated wrongly only if we have deserts which we are treated as lacking. Can the Kleinigian approach handle ill desert? We must not say that the innocent are treated unjustly because they are treated as they do not deserve, that is, are undeserving of punishment. However, we may say that those who are innocent deserve to be treated as such, and that they are not so treated if they are punished.[23] In general, where we might normally say that A has no deserts, but lacks Q and hence does not deserve treatment T, we may say instead that A possesses not-Q and deserves to be treated as such. The pitfall to be avoided if we employ the Kleinigian approach is the danger of thinking people have no (relevant) deserts when in fact they do.

If we reject the view that one and only one of the approaches is correct, then we might say that these different approaches offer us a choice of idiom. We might say that to argue that one view is right, the other wrong, is to misunderstand the nature of the issue. Suppose we accept that account of the conflict. Should we conclude that it matters little which idiom we adopt—as long as we are consistent and use only one idiom throughout? Certainly there is an intuitive appeal to the suggestion that we should adopt one idiom throughout. But it is not, I think, obvious that this is indeed the appropriate response. There are two dangers here: on the one hand

---

[22] This is the point I made earlier (2.1) with regard to compensation: although not compensating is necessary in order to treat a person as deserving to suffer, it is not sufficient.

[23] Sverdlik writes: 'I myself find it odd to say that X deserves not to be punished. It seems more proper to say that X does not deserve to be punished' (ibid. 322). It may be odd; but that only makes the point that we tend not to use the Kleinigian approach in the case of ill desert. It does not, of course, follow that we cannot.

there are the risks of confusion inherent in using incompatible idioms, on the other there is the danger of using one idiom throughout and thereby risking one of the pitfalls we have identified—of too rashly assuming on any occasion that a person has no (relevant) deserts, or of concluding too quickly that a particular action constitutes treating a person as a member of a particular class. By their nature these are difficult mistakes to avoid. Perhaps there is something to be said for using that idiom which, on any occasion, makes the argument we want to make most clearly, but to be willing to translate the argument into the other idiom, and to bear in mind both pitfalls we have identified, and, if there is a danger of confusion, to re-express the point in the language of fittingness—that is, in terms of treating people as lower or higher than they are.

The task of ensuring that we do not suppose people have no relevant deserts when they do is not made easier by the existence of another layer of confusing over-simplification stemming from our tendency to make precisely the opposite mistake: the mistake of supposing that people have deserts when they do not. This tendency exists because many of our uses of desert are in connection with what we may call 'discretionary practices': practices which are not required in order to avoid injustice (or unfitting treatment).

The awarding of examination grades is a discretionary practice. Many societies do grade by having examination systems, but a society in which there are no examinations, and thus no grades awarded, is not by that fact an unjust society. Indeed one might argue that such practices as grading and honouring in general are discretionary: they are practices which can be unjust, but which may be eschewed altogether without thereby doing any injustice. The classification of the practices of rewarding and punishing is particularly controversial here. The retributivist position is, in essence, that such practices must be available in order to avoid injustice. (At least in principle: if no one acts wrongly or rightly then no punishment or reward will be required.) If the retributivist is right, then punishing and rewarding are non-discretionary practices.

2. *Justice and Desert*   53

How ought we to use 'desert' when we are dealing with a discretionary practice? Our starting-point should be that treatment in accordance with a practice which is discretionary cannot in itself be deserved.[24] If such treatment were deserved, its denial would be unjust (or at least unfitting) and thus the practice would not be discretionary. If the practice of awarding a peace prize is discretionary—if a society which lacks such a practice is not thereby an unjust society—then no one can ever, strictly speaking, be said to deserve a peace prize. More controversially, if anti-retributivists are right and punishing and rewarding are discretionary—that is, a society which lacks the practices of rewarding and punishing is not thereby an unjust society—then no one ever deserves a reward or punishment.

Now as I have noted, discretionary practices, although not required in order to avoid acting unjustly (or unfittingly), are practices which can be performed unjustly (or unfittingly). Although we may not be required (on pain of acting unjustly or unfittingly) ever to honour anyone by awarding a peace prize (or to reward or punish if these are discretionary), if we do engage in such practices we must not do so unjustly (or unfittingly). Honours must not be given if so to act would be to treat recipients as other than they are. How is this to be expressed in the language of desert? We normally make the point by saying that honours must not be given where they are not deserved. But, strictly speaking, that will not do. If awarding a peace prize really is discretionary, then, strictly, no one ever deserves such an honour: such prizes are always not deserved.

I have claimed that there are two idioms in which cases where there is an absence of desert can be discussed: the Kleinigian and the Sverdlikian. I have claimed that, with care, either may be employed. If that is right, we should be able to discuss the relation of desert and discretionary practices in each of these idioms. We must now see if that is indeed possible.

---

[24] I leave aside here any arguments based on institutional entitlement and on comparative treatment.

On the Kleinigian account if people have no deserts, then they cannot be treated unfittingly no matter how they are treated. But, of course, it does not follow from the fact that people do not deserve to be honoured, say by receiving a peace prize, that they have no (relevant) deserts at all. Those who are unworthy of a peace prize deserve to be treated as such. We do not treat them as such by honouring. Thus what the unworthy deserve is not to be honoured. And if they are not treated in accordance with these deserts they will be treated unfittingly. By contrast those worthy of a peace prize do not merely not deserve a peace prize—the consequence of this practice being discretionary—they also do not deserve not to be honoured. In their case, then, neither honouring nor failing to honour is unjust (or unfitting).

On the Sverdlikian account we can be treated unjustly (or unfittingly) even if we have no deserts. We can be treated unjustly (or unfittingly) by being treated as having deserts we do not have. Now as I have noted, if the awarding of peace prizes is a discretionary practice, the worthy do not deserve to be so honoured. At first sight it may seem to follow that to honour the worthy would be unfitting for it would be to treat them as having deserts they do not have. But such an inference can be resisted. If awarding a peace prize is indeed discretionary and thus never, strictly, deserved, then to honour is not to treat as deserving the honour—although, of course, it is to act as one would need to act in order to treat as deserving to be honoured. Rather, strictly, to honour is to treat as not deserving not to be honoured. It is not true, then, even on the Sverdlikian account, that no one ever deserving an honour entails that honouring is always unjust (or unfitting).

Although these accounts may demonstrate that, with care, desert can be used coherently in the context of discretionary practices, they do not, I think, demonstrate that it can be so used with ease. (Nor is it only a matter of convenience. To congratulate someone appointed to a professorial chair by saying that no one less deserved not to have it might be mistaken for less than fulsome praise.) There is much to be said, then, in favour of making arguments in relation to discretionary practices in the idiom of fittingness, and of treating as higher or lower than is appropriate, rather than in the language of desert. Thus there would be some irony were rewarding and punishing to turn out to be discretionary practices, for in that case it will follow that the context in which desert is so often used—in connection with reward and punishment—is precisely the context in which its use is best eschewed if misunderstanding is to be avoided.

2.3 *The Revolt against Desert*

Although in popular moral thinking the appeal of desert remains very high, within political philosophy desert has been out of favour for much of this century. There has been something of a 'revolt against desert'.[25] This hostile mood towards desert has a number sources of varying degrees of sophistication. The most significant objection is probably that based on the claim that desert presupposes a responsibility we simply do not have. I will consider this objection to desert later (7.1–4). Here I want to discuss three objections which I will deal with more briefly: that desert is ineradicably vague—or, at least, too vague to determine what justice requires; that it is inherently inegalitarian; and that any pre-institutional desert presupposes pre-institutional status-affecting attributes, of which there are none.

Firstly, then, the issue of vagueness and indeterminacy. In contrast to entitlement (based either on a contract or on qualification under a rule), it seems often unclear, when we are deserving, what we are deserving of. Perhaps we believe that nurses are generally underpaid for the work they do, and believe they deserve more. But how much more would treat them according to their deserts? In essence this objection is that there is no satisfactory means of deriving what is deserved from the desert basis.

[25] Barry, *Political Argument*, 112.

Now I have argued (2.1) that *what* is deserved is determined by the requirement that all are to be treated in accordance with their status-affecting attributes—all are to be treated as members of the status classes to which they belong. We will fail to treat people in accordance with their deserts if we give expression to false beliefs regarding their status. If this is indeed so, then there is no question of what is deserved being radically undetermined. It is a mistake to suppose that there are no limits set on what is deserved stemming from the notion of desert itself.

Nevertheless, even if a charge of inherent radical indeterminacy can be rebutted, a more restrained indeterminacy charge can still be made. Given that only rarely is one particular form of treatment required in order to treat the deserver as a member a particular status class, or to express a belief that that deserver is a member of that class, what is deserved will rarely, if ever, be uniquely determined. Any one of an indefinitely large set of forms of treatment may be consistent with treating the deserver as having the desert basis in question.

This is, I think, a point about desert which must be acknowledged. But such indeterminacy is not peculiar to desert. It is, as we have seen, a feature of desert because it is a feature of treating, and it is a feature of treating because it is a feature of expression. There is no one-to-one correlation between a belief or judgement, and the means (words, gestures, actions, and so on) by which it is expressed. One might argue, then, that if it is appropriate to eschew the notion of desert on grounds of indeterminacy, it is appropriate to eschew the more general notion of expression. But the suggestion that we should avoid using the notion of expression seems absurd.

But perhaps it will be objected that the issue of the indeterminacy of desert is not an issue about desert *per se*, but desert in relation to justice. Justice, the argument might go, requires precision—we wish to know what exactly justice requires—and if desert will not deliver that precision, then desert is not the notion through which to explore what justice requires.

But this is an objection to the employment of desert only if the indeterminacy of desert is not replicated in justice. And surely indeterminacy is a feature of justice. It is highly implausible to suppose that justice always requires some unique mode of treatment. It is much more plausible to suppose that, although justice sets limits or side-constraints on what may be done— as many have noted, justice is the avoidance of injustice[26]— there are many differing arrangements and ways of acting, none of which are unjust.[27] The reply is, then, that although it is often not possible to determine what is uniquely required to treat in accordance with a desert claim, justice itself shares this indeterminacy. Such indeterminacy is, then, no ground on which to suppose that desert is not the concept on which to explicate what justice requires.

There is a further point. There are some practices which seem unquestionably unjust, others about which we are much less sure. In the first category we might place the punishment of the innocent, apartheid, and slavery; in the second the remuneration of any given work at a particular level. Now why should some practices seem so clearly unjust, others much less so? The explanation, I suggest, is that practices are clearly unjust where the meaning of the action is least open to question. On some occasions what justice requires may be more precisely determined than on others. The fact that desert and expression sometimes, but only sometimes, have an indeterminacy is one reason why this is so.

I turn now to a second source of reluctance to appeal to desert: the belief that desert is inherently inegalitarian. (This is, of course, only an objection to desert for egalitarians; but many espouse egalitarianism.) How should we view the relationship between the notions of desert and equality? Is there indeed such a connection that egalitarians must, or at least should, eschew desert?

---

[26] See F. A. Hayek, *Law, Legislation and Liberty* (London, 1976), ii. 36 and 162–4 n. 9, and Lucas, *On Justice*, 4, including n. 7, for references to places where this point has been made.

[27] Cf. Rawls, *A Theory of Justice*, 201.

The association of desert with inequality is not an unreasonable one. There seems no doubt that there is a tendency to associate desert with inequality in political, if not in philosophical, debate. Firstly, desert is the concept of choice for those who wish to defend the justice of unequal distribution and treatment. (Distributing according to need may call for an unequal allocation of resources, but the justice of such a distribution is often viewed as a means to the achievement of an equality of welfare.) Inequalities can be defended if desert bases can be shown to be unequal; in the absence of a willingness to claim that there is a natural aristocracy, and to deny that, at the most fundamental level, all have an equal status, these unequal desert bases will refer to what people have done, rather than what they are. Secondly, as I discuss later (7.4), there is a tendency to associate desert exclusively with reward and punishment. Although in theory rewards and punishments might be equally deserved, this is, of course, highly unlikely to occur in practice. A distribution which aims to reward and punish is almost certain to be an unequal distribution. Desert, through its close association with rewarding and punishing, may thus take on an aura of inequality.

But is desert really inegalitarian? And should the very notion of desert be rejected by egalitarians? The fact that desert is often used to defend unequal distribution does not, of course, show that there is anything inegalitarian about desert itself. Desert may be used in both inegalitarian and egalitarian arguments. If the ground or grounds on which people deserve to be treated—the desert bases—vary from one person to another, then different people may deserve different treatment. But where a relevant desert base is possessed in equal measure people do not merely not deserve different treatment, but deserve not to be treated differently.[28]

---

[28] This point is made by Nagel: 'I am suggesting that for many benefits and disadvantages, certain characteristics of the recipient are relevant to what he deserves. If people are equal in the relevant respects, that by itself constitutes a reason to distribute the benefit to them equally' (Thomas Nagel, 'Equal Treatment and Compensatory Discrimination', in Marshall Cohen, Thomas Nagel, and Thomas Scanlon (eds.), *Equality and Preferential Treatment* (Princeton, 1977), 9).

Indeed I want to suggest that for egalitarians to eschew the notion of desert is perverse, for there is good reason to view desert as the most appropriate notion for expressing what egalitarianism is. Egalitarianism is not simply a view of *how* people should be treated (namely, as equals), but a view about *why* they should be treated in a particular way. The egalitarian holds that people should be treated as equals because they are equal. But, as we have seen, such a relation between the status of a being and treatment which expresses that status is precisely the relation embodied in desert. It may be that egalitarians also hold that all have a right to treatment as an equal; but we should not identify an egalitarian with someone who holds such a view, for we may believe that people have a right to be treated as equals without holding that they are equals.[29]

Finally, what of the claim that there are no pre-institutional status-affecting attributes on which to base any pre-institutional desert, and thus, when we are concerned with justice, we should focus on what has been qualified for under existing (not unjust) institutions, that is, with entitlements. We may agree that *some* attributes are status-affecting only because of the existence of particular institutions—or, at least, some reasons for an attribute being status-affecting may be institution-dependent. To illustrate: what makes someone a good lawyer will, we may expect, be determined, at least in part, by the nature of existing legal institutions and practices. It is to be expected that the attributes which make for a good lawyer in a legal system which emphasizes conciliation and reconciliation will be different from those required in an adversarial

---

[29] Someone who believes, say, that the members of two races are of unequal status, but who has, in order to comply with a condition set by God for entrance into a land of abundance, been a party to a contract to treat all, irrespective of race, as equals, is hardly an egalitarian. Such a person may hold that all have a right to treatment as equals, but that all are not equals. The inappropriateness of the notion of a right to characterize egalitarianism reflects the conclusory nature of rights, and the diverse sources of rights. (I borrow the term 'conclusory' from John Finnis, *Natural Law and Natural Rights* (Oxford, 1980), 211.) Egalitarianism must be characterized in non-conclusory terms if it is to be characterized, at least in part, by specific reasons for action. Desert is not conclusory.

system. But the issue is whether *all* status-affecting attributes must be institutionally dependent, and this seems extremely doubtful. The attributes of the good lawyer are institution-based since to be a lawyer is to have a certain role, and that role exists within a practice which embodies institutions. As we move away from contexts where a description in terms of roles is appropriate we may expect that it will be increasingly plausible to view status-affecting attributes as institutionally independent. Suppose we believe that we—or God—have a certain status on account of being free and rational, wise and powerful, loving and reliable, and so on. It is hard to see why we need accept that such attributes affect status only on account of the existence of some particular set of institutions.

2.4 *Justice as Desert: The Problem Cases*

I have argued that to accept justice as fittingness is to accept that desert is central to justice, that we shall avoid acting unjustly if only we treat all in accordance with their deserts. Thus to defend the claim that justice is a member of the fittingness family of concepts we must argue that treating in accordance with desert is not merely a requirement for acting justly: we must argue that justice is exclusively concerned with desert.

Now certainly there are problem cases for this view, and to defend the claim that justice is exclusively concerned with desert these cases need to be dealt with. Let us take stock of which cases these are. Firstly, there are, it seems, considerations often thought relevant to justice which cannot, without impropriety, be expressed in terms of desert. These include need and entitlement.[30] The view that a just distribution is, sometimes or in part, a distribution according to need has

---

[30] Cf.: 'I have attempted to separate the common notion of justice into three elements. Each of the criteria which have been distinguished—rights, deserts and needs—forms a part of that notion, and each is irreducible to the others' (Miller, *Social Justice*, 151).

some appeal.[31] Those who hold that justice (at least some-times) requires a distribution of resources according to need may not (and generally do not) suppose that need is status-affecting, that to be in need is to be more (or less) worthy of admiration or respect.[32] A similar point can be made with regard to entitlement—that is, claims based on promises or contracts, or on qualification under some general rule or prac-tice. Being promised, or qualifying under a rule, is not gener-ally supposed to be status-affecting. The status requirement, then, explains why it is (usually) inappropriate to offer need and entitlement as bases of desert.

Secondly, there are, as we have seen, considerations which are normally expressed in the language of desert, but which pose difficulties for the account of desert I have sought to defend. Claims to deserve on the basis of contribution, and to deserve compensation when one suffers through no fault of one's own, seem, on the face of it, often to violate the status requirement.

The problem, then, is to deal with these apparent counter-examples to the account of justice I have proposed, and

---

[31] See Lucas, *On Justice*, 164–5 n. 6 for a number of writers who have allowed distribution according to need as a precept of justice.

[32] Cf.: 'What disqualifies needs from being taken as grounds for desert is . . . that no one wishes to have them or admires others for having them' (Miller, *Social Justice*, 86).

Miller offers a second reason: '(for most needs) everyone has them until they are satisfied' (ibid.). But this ground seems implausible. Rationality may be almost universal amongst humans but that is no reason to suppose it is not a ground of respect and desert.

Galston offers a different argument for the claim that need cannot func-tion as a desert basis: 'If f is to serve as a desert-basis, it is a necessary con-dition that x, the treatment appropriate to it, be accorded the same normative or moral evaluation as f. If f is regarded as good or desirable, so is x, and similarly if f is regarded as bad. Clearly, need does not satisfy this criterion; it is regarded as undesirable but the treatment to which it gives rise is considered desirable' (Galston, *Justice and the Human Good*, 174). But it is not clear why this 'necessary condition' should be accepted. If it is simply a generalization about the use of 'desert', the argument is vulnerable to counter-examples. I have argued already (1.4) that superior status need not always be marked by more favourable treatment. In any case the argument here can simply be turned on its head, and need offered as a counter-example. On the other hand, if it is more than a generalization it is not clear how it is to be defended.

thereby offer a defence of that account. Dealing with these problem cases occupies much of the next three chapters. In Chapter 3 I discuss need, contribution, and compensation, in Chapters 4 and 5 entitlements based on promises and on qualification under rules respectively. I shall employ a number of strategies in attempting to defuse these apparent counter-examples, but the general form of one in particular I want to introduce here. This is the strategy of developing a reductive argument, employing the notion of indirect desert.

The standard argument against the view that justice is concerned only with desert is, as we have seen, based on the claim that there are considerations relevant to justice which cannot (or do not) function as desert bases—such considerations not being status-affecting. This objection will be defused if it is possible to develop a reductive argument of the following kind. Suppose it is said that justice requires that A be treated in accordance with X, but that X cannot function as a desert basis. Now from this it does not follow that A cannot deserve in accordance with X, for there may be some status-affecting attribute of A, Y, such that, to treat A in accordance with Y it is necessary to treat A in accordance with X. If, for example, there is some status-affecting attribute (or set of attributes) of people, call it D, such that to treat people in accordance with D it is necessary to treat them in accordance with their needs, then we may say that people deserve (albeit indirectly) to be treated in accordance with their needs, even though need is not functioning (and cannot function) as a desert basis. In short, it does not follow from the fact that X is not a possible desert basis that a person cannot deserve to be treated in accordance with X. To suppose that it does is to overlook the possibility of indirect desert.

Whether any particular claim is to be understood as an indirect desert claim depends, at least in part, on the plausibility of the implied desert basis, and on the plausibility of alternative (and especially conflicting) descriptions of the justification for the treatment in question. To be sure the mere possibility of an argument based on indirect desert is insufficient to show that the consideration in question is (albeit indirectly) based on desert. But neither should the possibility of such an account be overlooked.

The defence of justice as fittingness requires, then, the completion of a programme, a programme of eliminating, or reducing to desert, those considerations which seem relevant to justice, but which resist expression in terms of desert. In completing such a programme we may hope not only to defend an account of the concept of justice, but to illuminate the underlying rationale of a number of precepts of justice.

3

Members, Wholes, and Partners

HOW should we view the relation between the individual and society? This is, perhaps, the central question of social and political philosophy. Political philosophies differ radically in their conception of this relation. At one extreme is the view that individuals are mere parts of a greater social whole in the way that limbs are members of a body; at the other is the view that individuals are radically separate and complete in themselves. In this chapter I want to consider how our view of this relationship can be expected to affect our view of what justice requires.

A number of precepts intended to determine a proper distribution of benefits and burdens between individuals may be understood as ways of giving expression to (what is viewed as being) the relationship between the individual and the social union of which the individual is a part (if any). So at least I shall argue. I begin by examining precepts (for distributing benefits and burdens, and compensation) which may be understood as means by which we may treat as a member, and as a complete being, a whole. Next I turn to precepts which may be viewed as expressing partnership, which I take to include elements of both membership and wholeness. Finally, I turn to the question of whether these precepts are to be considered principles of justice, and if so, whether they are compatible with justice as fittingness. The chapter begins, then, the defence of the account of justice I want to offer. In so doing it seeks to explain how certain considerations often thought relevant to justice can, without impropriety, be expressed in the language of desert.

3.1 Treating as a Member and as a Whole

How should we view the relationship between the individual and society? Consider first the view that individuals are members of a society in the way that limbs are parts of a body. On this view the individual is exclusively a member, engulfed by the society, the social whole, of which it is a mere part. To view ourselves as exclusively members is to see ourselves, considered alone, as fragments, as incomplete.[1] A very different view is that individuals are essentially separate, and society is merely a collection of those individuals. Here it is the individual, rather than society, which is viewed as the whole. I want to look at these two conceptions of the relationship between the individual and society, and at the means by which conceptions of that relationship may be expressed. I begin with the view that we are exclusively members.

What institutional arrangements would give expression to membership? To conceive of people exclusively as members of a social whole is to conceive of them as lacking independent interests (a good) of their own. (We do not suppose that limbs have interests independent of the body of which they are members.) The distributive principles which express that we are exclusively members must reflect this.

A precept expressing membership is the principle of allocating benefits and burdens according to the interests of the (social) whole. If individuals are not the bearers of independent interests, no distributive principle can be based on individuals' interests, it is the interests of the whole which are to be promoted. Each member is to be held liable to contribute to the good of the whole according to the ability of the member. Given differing abilities, members will be expected to contribute in different ways, and their contributions may be

---

[1] Although 'member' may not always suggest the incompleteness which the use of 'part' would imply, 'member' is used in contexts where the focus is on the larger whole, such as when we speak of people as members of parliament, religious orders, sporting teams, or the cast of a play. This use also respects the etymology of 'member', which comes from the Latin *membrum*, a limb.

of differing values. Those with greater skills, or greater wealth, will be expected to contribute more. We have, then, a principle of from each according to ability, to each according to need, but both ability and need are to be understood by reference to the interests of the whole.

Is there any place here for the practice of compensating? If by compensation we understand a benefit provided to someone who has suffered, with the intention of returning the sufferer to (or towards) the level of well-being experienced before the loss, then it would seem not, for such an account of compensation has individual differentiation and interests embodied in it. (We can identify the level of a member's well-being only if we suppose that members have interests.) If, however, we suppose that the fundamental idea of compensation is of counter-balancing, then just as we speak of one part of a body compensating for another (as when a person with weak eyesight may have highly developed hearing), so we might suppose that one member may develop strengths to counter-balance the weaknesses of others, and we might suppose that members, *qua* members, have a duty to develop such strengths. (Such a principle of compensation—if that is what it is—may be viewed as a particular instance of the general principle for distributing burdens applicable: we are liable according to our ability to contribute to the interests of the social whole.)

The antithesis of the claim that each of us is exclusively a member is the claim that we are not parts at all but are complete in ourselves. Individuals are separate and whole. How is this exclusive wholeness of the individual to be expressed? How may individuals be treated as wholes?

To be alive is to be at risk. We may control what happens to us to some extent, but we remain very much at the mercy of fortune, good or ill. We may have a life of good health or be struck down by accident or disease. We may have just those natural talents which society requires or we may not; we may stumble upon a valuable invention or the most rationally planned research may lead down a blind alley. Now one way to express that we are separate wholes is to suppose that we each have our own particular relation with fortune, and to adopt distributive precepts which respect these individual fates. By refraining from disturbing each individual's fate we give expression to our distinctness, our separation, and our wholeness.

How are individual fates to be respected? Consider, first, cases of allocating benefits between those who have not contributed to their production. The distribution of an estate between offspring, or the distribution of (virgin) land between (all) individuals might be considered cases of this type. Here an equal division of the benefit may be viewed as a means of expressing not only our equality but also our separate wholeness. Such a distribution is likely to be unequal in its effects on individuals, at least where the needs and interests of recipients vary. By ignoring variations in needs and effects we treat them as differences we have no business in redressing. In so far as these differences are a reflection of the individual fortunes of each we thereby respect individual fates, and express the wholeness of each.

In cases of allocation such as these there is, or need be, little or no interaction between people. But in many cases there will be interaction and the question arises how benefits and burdens are to be distributed when there is such interaction, if the objective is to express the wholeness of each. Consider the distribution of the benefits of joint production. How are benefits to be distributed if the objective is to respect individual fates? Here the appropriate precept is the principle of distributing benefits according to contribution. To apply this principle is to attempt to unravel or disentangle the process of joint production in such a way as to leave the risks of life with the individual.[2] The differing benefits arising from individual fortune are returned to the individual. Thus if leaving all with the benefits of their own particular good and ill fortune is a means of expressing the separateness and the wholeness of each person, then so too is the extension of this approach to

---

[2] Cf. Robert Nozick, *Anarchy, State and Utopia* (Oxford, 1974), 185–6.

the distribution of the benefits and burdens generated in societies whose processes of production are highly integrated. What of the distribution of burdens? Treating as an exclusive whole will, presumably, preclude imposing burdens on some for the benefit of others, or for the benefit of any supposed social whole. A principle which is consistent with treating as an exclusive whole (and which also avoids treating as a mere tool or means) is the principle of requiring from each only what each chooses to contribute.[3] This may, however, be to err on the side of caution: it may be possible to impose some burdens (without consent) without treating as a member (or as a tool). If burdens are inevitable, or their imposition is permissible (perhaps to provide public goods), then an equal division of the burden—as by a poll tax, say—will be consistent with treating each as a separate whole.[4] (If, at least, we assume that each is not only a whole but is equal in other status-affecting attributes.) As with distributing benefits, such a division is likely to be unequal in its effects: a heavier burden will be placed on those less able to contribute, a lighter burden on the more fortunate. If the aim is to treat each as an exclusive whole by respecting each individual's fate, this is not, of course, an objection. Quite the reverse: it is essential if the aim is to be achieved.

Turning to compensation we may argue that the notion of unravelling also underlies practices of compensation where the aim is to give expression to the exclusive wholeness of the individual, by respecting individual fates. (Once again, then, compensation may be seen as a particular application of the principles underlying more general distributive precepts.)

[3] Cf.: 'From each according to what he chooses to do . . .' (ibid. 160).

[4] The charge that such a principle treats each as a tool or part can be denied if the pooled resources are used for the benefit of all, for we do not treat a being as a tool if we act in a manner intended to promote its interests, even if we act contrary to its will. Even a charge of paternalism may be denied if contribution for public good provision is irrational from the individual perspective. Enforcement of such a principle may not restrict individual freedom (albeit for the individual's own good), so much as enable individuals to achieve ends they may wish to achieve but, acting as (rational) individuals, cannot.

Individuals, as wholes, are the bearers of interests, and the aim of compensation now is to provide benefits to an individual who has suffered a loss or injury with a view to returning that individual to the level of welfare which would have been experienced but for that loss or injury.

In what circumstances is such compensation for suffering due? The precept governing compensation which treats individuals as exclusive wholes is the view that compensation is due when and only when one person's suffering is the fault of another or others. This approach to compensation expresses the wholeness of each person in two ways. Firstly, the principle embodies the idea that we are responsible—can be called to account—for the costs of what we do and fail to do. But the principle goes further and asserts that there should be compensation *only* where an agent is at fault. It goes on, then, to assert that, once again, the risks of life should be allowed to lie where they fall. This principle, like distribution according to contribution, is an attempt to unravel affairs when there is interaction, and in a manner which respects individual fates; following this principle provides each with the winnings and losses of an individual game of chance with fortune. Thereby, again, our wholeness is expressed.

3.2 Treating as a Partner

If we wish to reject both exclusive membership and exclusive wholeness as one-sided, we will want to consider whether we can view ourselves as *both* wholes and members. Can the individual exist neither engulfed nor radically separated, being complete and whole while at the same time a member of something larger? I shall assume that *partnership* involves this notion of partial whole.[5] In this way we may consider the

---

[5] Cf. 'But each of us is not only a part but also a "system" or a whole. That we are parts does not entail that we are not also wholes; and men—unlike atoms—are what were once called "partial wholes", parts of a greater whole which are themselves wholes with parts of their own' (Jonathan Barnes, 'Partial Wholes', *Social Philosophy and Policy*, 8 (1990), 2).

It has been claimed that a 'rhythm of primitive whole, fragmentation, and

requirements for treating as a partial whole by considering a familiar concept. In partnerships (we may think of business and bridge partnerships, marriages, and so on) there is, of course, a union, and partners are members of a greater whole. But the partner need not be engulfed, and when we speak of a partnership the focus may be on both the union and the constituent elements of that union. Individuality and differentiation—in the ideal, at least—may be preserved in partnership.

If we are to think of ourselves as partners, we must conceive of ourselves both as individual wholes and as members of a social whole (the partnership). And, if we are to be treated as such, we must find forms of treatment which give expression to both aspects of partnership. Now if we are partners, then we are members—not *only* members, but still members. Thus to view ourselves as partners is to accept that there is a whole (the partnership) which has interests, and to which we, as partners, have a duty to contribute. Nevertheless, partners are also to be considered wholes, and with interests of their own. There is, then, the possibility, indeed the likelihood, that the interests of individual partners will not always coincide with the interests of the partnership. It seems reasonable, however, to say that as we suppose any conflict between the partners' and the partnership's interests to increase so our willingness to believe in the possibility of genuine partnership must decrease. If there is to be a partnership at all, then the interests of the individual members will need some degree of coincidence with the interests of the partnership. That, it seems, is part of what is required in order to view partnership as a synthesis.

reunification asserts itself widely in Western thought. It beats not only in Hegel and . . . in Marx but in much religious doctrine, in the Christian triad of innocence, fall and redemption, in Aristophanes' account of love in Plato's *Symposium*, in some psychoanalytic narrations of the genesis of the person, and . . . throughout Schiller's *Letters on the Aesthetic Education of Mankind*' (G. A. Cohen, *Karl Marx's Theory of History: A Defence* (Oxford, 1978), 21). If the notions of membership and wholeness correspond to the stages of primitive whole and fragmentation, partnership may be viewed as the synthesis corresponding to reunification.

Suppose, then, that there is a sufficient coincidence of interests for partnership to be possible. How is that partnership to find expression? As we have seen, one way to express our wholeness is through institutional arrangements which respect and emphasize individual destinies, individual fortunes. Now it is clear that *this* means of expressing the wholeness of the individual is simply unavailable if we are to treat one another as partners, for to be in partnership is, to some degree at least, to share a common fate. The question arises, then, whether there is some other means of treating as a whole, a means which can be adopted within the context of a partnership.

I want to argue that the principle of distributing according to individual need (and a corresponding principle for contribution) may be interpreted as an attempt to express both the union and the differentiation, the membership and the wholeness, which constitute partnership. I shall not claim that they are necessarily successful for what is required to treat as a partner is a particularly complex issue, adding the ambiguities and complexities inherent in the notion of partnership itself to those stemming from the expression of a being's nature through action. What I do claim, however, is that a reasonable case can be made for saying that the principle of need gives expression to both membership and wholeness, and that such a rationale for the principle of need makes sense of features of that principle which call for explanation.

I want to begin by considering how we should understand the principle of distribution according to individual need. Distributing according to need is often supposed by its adherents to be a principle of justice. If we assume that the principle is indeed a principle of justice, then it may seem plausible to interpret the principle as requiring distribution in *proportion* to need. Perhaps resources should be distributed in proportion to need so that the greater the need the greater the resources allocated; or perhaps we should focus on the effects on need satisfaction of a particular distribution of resources, and distribute available resources in such a manner as will satisfy the highest equal proportion of each person's needs. (We might find, then, that with available resources the highest proportion of each person's needs which can be satisfied is, say, 60 per cent.)

But, I want to argue, we should reject both of these interpretations, and indeed the claim that proportionality has any role to play. The principle of distributing according to need (when viewed as a principle of justice) is most plausible when it is interpreted as the principle that those who are in greatest (non-self-inflicted) need have first claim on whatever resources are considered available. No resources should be devoted to the less needy (on grounds of need) if they are already in less need than the need in which those in greater need will be left.[6] I will refer to this as the principle of greatest need, first claim (or GNFC). Adopting this view we are to satisfy the needs of those in greatest need until their level of need is equal to those in next greatest need, then satisfy the needs of members of both groups until remaining needs are equal to those in next greatest need, and so on.[7]

How can the adoption of the principle of distribution according to need, interpreted as GNFC, be defended? It may be said that, wherever possible, need should be reduced, for

[6] This is an argument against proportionality. But I also want to question what I take to be the argument for proportionality. I want to suggest that the appeal of proportionality may be spurious in this context. Proportionality may be thought to have a role in distribution according to need (as a principle of justice) because there is a tendency to associate justice and proportionality. Now to be sure justice may often require proportionality, for treatment given may need to be proportional to the desert basis where the desert basis may vary in degree. The classic example is the claim that punishment is just only if it is in proportion to the wrongdoing to which it is a response. It is supposed that there are degrees of wrongdoing (the desert basis), and that the treatment deserved must vary in response. Now if need were a desert basis, this argument would apply in the case of need. But as we have seen, need does not satisfy the status requirement, and thus there is good reason to believe that need cannot function as a desert basis (2.4). This does not rule out the possibility of defending proportionality, but it does count against any easy presumption in favour of proportionality based on an association of justice and proportionality.

[7] I leave aside here the problems raised when the function relating resources to need satisfaction is discontinuous and where to make any improvement in the position of those in greatest need is to make their level of need less than those in next greatest need.

(genuine) need is an evil. But such an argument falls short of justifying the distinctive features of the GNFC principle: if it is simply the evil of unsatisfied needs with which we are concerned, it is hard to see why we should endorse the GNFC principle rather than the principle of distributing resources so as to minimize the number of unsatisfied needs (or units of unsatisfied need).[8]

To adopt the principle that unsatisfied need should be minimized is to take what is, in essentials, a utilitarian view. As such, the principle might be derived from the principle of maximizing happiness on the basis of an empirical claim that to minimize unsatisfied need maximizes happiness, or it may be defended as a form of utilitarianism in its own right by adopting the particular theory of the good that an unsatisfied need is intrinsically bad. This principle can be supported by the kind of argument applicable to utilitarianism generally: we identify what has value or disvalue (defending this claim when necessary) and argue that we ought to act so as to maximize value. To defend the principle as not unjust we must then argue that following such a principle does not treat anyone as less than he or she is. Certainly the principle of minimizing unsatisfied need seems to satisfy any requirement to treat all as worthy of equal concern. (To paraphrase Bentham, to follow this principle is to allow each person's unit of need to count for one, and no one's for more than one.)

There is no denying the appeal of acting so as to minimize the number of unsatisfied needs (or units of unsatisfied need). By contrast, adopting GNFC will mean being willing to act in a way which reduces need less than is possible.[9] Clearly, this

[8] A different principle (equivalent in its effect only where the number of needs is a constant) would be to maximize the number of satisfied needs (or units of satisfied need). But I take it that this is a less plausible principle, for it seems doubtful that there is the same value in the satisfaction of needs which we first create and then satisfy as there is in the satisfaction of naturally occurring needs.

[9] GNFC is not equivalent to need minimization. If, with available resources, a hospital is able either to prevent a one-legged man losing his only leg, or 100 two-legged men each losing one leg, then GNFC will require that the man in danger of losing his only leg is to be treated first. But if we are to minimize (units of) unsatisfied need, then we must try to weigh the

requires a defence. We might suppose that an argument from equality is available. As we have seen, the adoption of GNFC will mean that (where the allocation of resources is useful, that is, does indeed assist in the satisfaction of need) resources are allocated first to those in greatest need until they are equal in need to those in next greatest need, then to the needs of all these individuals until they are equal to those in next greatest need, and so on. The effect of repeated applications of GNFC, we might argue, will be a tendency to an equality of welfare. We might, therefore, suppose that the argument for GNFC rests on an argument from equality.

But there are difficulties with such an argument. Firstly, it assumes that a satisfactory justification for equalizing welfare is available. Secondly, the argument relies on a particular interpretation of equality which is not beyond question. The argument assumes that the appropriate measure of the degree of inequality in any group is the spread between those in greatest need and those in least need. If we adopt a different measure of inequality—say the standard deviation of need in the group—then it may be that by focusing resources on the most needy (where these needs are relatively expensive to satisfy) inequality is not reduced as much as it might be by a different allocation. Thirdly, if the most effective way to improve the position of those in greatest need is by providing incentives to those who are in less need, then a first concern for those in greatest need may, in practice, entail *increasing* the spread of inequalities of need, for it may result in the reduction of the needs of those in less need more than the needs of those in greater need.[10] Thus equalizing welfare and GNFC may conflict.

A more plausible basis for distribution according to need, interpreted as GNFC, derives from understanding the greater needs of the few against the lesser needs of the many. Nor does there seem any reason to suppose that minimizing (units of) unsatisfied need will lead to a distribution of resources in proportion to need, or to any given proportion of people's needs being satisfied. Need minimization requires that the cheapest needs be satisfied first. There seems no reason to suppose that this will result in any proportionality.

[10] Cf. John Rawls, *A Theory of Justice* (Oxford, 1972), sect. 13.

principle as a means of treating as a partner, as both a whole and a member. The objection to utilitarianism that it 'does not take seriously the distinction between persons'[11] can be made against the principle of minimizing need: in failing to mark the distinction between people, it fails to express their separation and, by implication, their wholeness. To distribute according to need, understood as GNFC, is to consider each person separately. And once we consider each person and their claim separately there is force in the idea that the person in the greatest need has the first claim, a claim which is unaffected by whether needs are to be found amongst others in such a way that it is possible to remove more needs by attending to the less needy. The adoption of such a decision procedure, particularly in cases where the consequences of adopting GNFC diverge significantly from those of adopting the minimization of need, involving as it does a refusal to 'add up', asserts that individuals are not mere parts, and is, then, a means of giving expression to the fact that each person is a whole.[12]

But the principle of need gives expression not simply to wholeness; it is also a means of expressing the fact that each partner is a member. To the extent that our needs are not self-inflicted, a distribution according to need is a means by which we may nullify accidents and the natural lottery, and share each other's fate. It is, thereby, a means of expressing our union.

We may doubt that the distribution according to need required to express partnership extends to needs which are

---

[11] Rawls, *A Theory of Justice*, 27. See also pp. 187–9, and Nozick, *Anarchy, State and Utopia*, 33.

[12] It would seem that this argument is not available to Rawls, for although he emphasizes our fundamental separation from each other, in isolation we are not complete: 'Only in the social union is the individual complete' (Rawls, *A Theory of Justice*, 525n.). But if we are not complete, it is hard to see why we should be thought to be done an injustice by processes which add up. Even if we allow that we are being treated as not separate when we are, it would still need to be explained why such treatment is unjust. Certainly, being separated is not generally considered to be status-enhancing.

self-inflicted. Firstly, given the degree of coincidence of interests required for partnership, any infliction of need on the self is likely to result in the infliction of need on the partnership. Self-infliction of need is thus likely to tend to undermine the existence of any partnership, and thus any claim to be a partner. Secondly, needs which are genuinely self-inflicted are hardly a part of that individual's *fate*. Thus facing nature with a common front, or sharing one another's fate, does not require distributing on the basis of self-inflicted need. Thirdly, failing to hold each responsible for needs which are self-inflicted may, plausibly, be viewed not simply as a way of failing to express wholeness, but as an expression that the individual is not a whole. (Membership requires that we share our fates, but wholeness requires that we take responsibility for what we do as individuals.) For these reasons we may argue that the rationale for the principle of need, based on the expression of partnership, does not extend to self-inflicted needs.

I have argued that a rationale for distributing according to need, understood as GNFC, is to treat as a partner. The GNFC principle does not rest only on treating as a whole and a member. Another premiss of this argument is equality of status: the principle of GNFC assumes that all are equal in the sense that the needs of each are of equal concern. If the person in greatest need is to have first claim irrespective of who he or she is, equality of concern is presupposed.[13] But, clearly, equality of status alone is insufficient for a defence of GNFC: as we have noted, the principle of minimizing unsatisfied need also treats each as worthy of equal concern. The requirement that people be treated as equals is insufficient to provide any reason to prefer the principle of GNFC to need minimization. What grounds the adoption of GNFC, in preference to need minimization, is the expression of wholeness in the context of partnership.

---

[13] Cf.: 'if the satisfaction of needs is seen as a matter of justice, [an] underlying premiss is required. The premiss is difficult to state with clarity, but it may be expressed by saying that every man is as worthy of respect as every other. That is to say there is an underlying equality' (David Miller, *Social Justice* (Oxford, 1976), 146).

What of the distribution of burdens? Once again the necessary principle, if it is to be an expression of partnership, must express the wholeness of each where there is a sharing of fortune. An equal distribution of burdens, such as a poll tax, is to be rejected as inconsistent with a sharing of fortune and the expression of a common destiny. The distribution of burdens in a partnership must reflect the ability of the individual to shoulder those burdens, in so far as this ability stems from events for which the individual partner is not responsible. If those who have abilities (as a result of fortune) are not expected to share the benefits of those abilities, they are not treated as members of a union; and a principle of distribution which does not reflect individual inability (as a result of misfortune) treats those who are less able as non-members.

But the requirement that individuals are to be treated as wholes sets limits on the extent to which burdens may be imposed. To sacrifice the interests of any particular individual for the interests of the social whole is to treat that individual as a member only, not as a partner. A principle for distributing burdens which treats individuals as partners will be one which is defensible taking each partner separately: there must be no adding up in the process of justification. (In any case, if the individual is not to be treated as a mere tool or means, the burdens, or at least the institutions taken together, must either be in the individual's interests, or subject to the individual's consent.) Again, then, there is reason to suppose that a partnership will require a significant measure of coincidence between the interests of different partners, and of the partnership.

Finally, what of compensation in a partnership? I have suggested that a person viewed exclusively as a member may have a duty to compensate for the failings of others (that is, other members), irrespective of whether there has been action or a failure to act by the member. By contrast a person viewed exclusively as a whole has a duty to provide compensation only where, as a result of an action or a failure to act, that person is to be held responsible for the loss. This principle of compensation which treats each as an exclusive whole rests, I argued, on two claims: that we should be held responsible for making good losses which are our fault; and that the risks of life (for which no one is to be called to account) should be allowed to lie where they fall.

Now whereas allowing risks to lie where they fall is *a* means of expressing wholeness, and one which we may replace (and in partnership must replace), it seems plausible to suppose that being held responsible for what is our fault is necessary if we are to be treated as a whole. (I assumed that this was so when I argued that self-inflicted needs may not be covered by a principle of distribution according to need expressing partnership.) If this is so, then responsibility for actions and failures to act (as individuals) will be preserved in partnership, and compensation will be due when, say, one partner injures the interests of another. (This is not to say that the duty should be enforced: there is a place for charity and mercy within partnerships.)

In partnership, however, the claim that no compensation is due for those who suffer through no one's fault must be rejected. This is required if partners are to face nature with a common front and share one another's fate. Partnership is expressed, then, in a system where compensation is due for losses for which others can be called to account, but also those whose suffering is simply misfortune. Once again, compensation is, it seems, based on the same principles as distribution generally.[14]

We have seen how a number of precepts governing the distribution of benefits and burdens can be understood as giving expression to the relationship between the individual and the

---

[14] It might be argued that there should be no compensation for losses which are no one's fault where those who suffer those losses are in less need than those whose position cannot be improved with the resources available under a principle of GNFC. Although this seems the more coherent position, it has the disadvantage that it is likely to restrict significantly the opportunities we have to express common membership with our partners, and the number of partners to whom we have the opportunity to express our solidarity, for adopting GNFC may result in a very high proportion of resources being devoted to a small number of members. (Where there is fault, and compensation is due as an expression of wholeness rather than membership, this issue will not arise.)

social whole; in particular they may be viewed as means by which membership and wholeness may be expressed. I do not claim that these precepts are either entirely or exclusively successful in expressing membership and wholeness.[15] Such claims cannot be made on the basis of the brief discussion I have given here. My claim is rather that the problem of expressing membership and wholeness provides the background against which these precepts are to be understood, and, as such, the background against which to consider the relationship between these precepts and justice. And it is to this issue—the relationship between these precepts and justice, and, in particular, the account of justice I have sought to defend—that I now turn.

3.3 *Members, Wholes, Partners, and Justice*

Are the various precepts we have discussed precepts of *justice*? Would we, in endorsing any of these precepts, thereby be indicating our view of what justice requires? It is sometimes supposed that any distributive principle is, *ipso facto*, a principle of justice. If we take this view, then the precepts we have discussed which express membership, wholeness, and partnership will indeed be principles of justice. This is to identify the concept of justice by reference to a particular issue, the

---

[15] I have argued that adopting the principle of GNFC may be viewed as a way of treating as a partner, but I am not suggesting that the adoption of this principle is necessary in order to treat as a partner. Rawls's two principles are offered as a means by which we may express our partnership. The principles are supposed to express our membership: 'In justice as fairness men agree to share one another's fate' (Rawls, *A Theory of Justice*, 102); and 'The difference principle . . . does seem to correspond to a natural meaning of fraternity . . .' (ibid. 105). But we are not to be treated simply as members: it is important 'to take seriously the plurality and distinctness of individuals' (ibid. 29); the persons in the original position are to be thought of as 'independent' (ibid. 252); given the requirement of unanimity each has a veto over the choice of principles; and there is an eschewal of adding up: 'The question of attaining the greatest net balance of satisfactions never arises in justice as fairness . . . ' (ibid. 30).

issue of how benefits and burdens are to be distributed.[16] I have rejected the view that justice is essentially distributive (1.4), and have claimed that justice is to be understood by reference to a particular type of reason for action (1.2). In distributing benefits and burdens we may act unjustly: acting justly requires that certain distributive practices are avoided. But it does not follow that all distributive principles are necessarily principles of justice. I claim, then, that we should leave open the possibility of our endorsing some or all of these distributive precepts without implying that they are our principles of justice.

What of the relationship between these precepts and the account of justice I have offered? Are these precepts, when they are adopted as a matter of justice, compatible with justice as fittingness? To accept justice as fittingness is to be committed to the view that, in so far as these precepts are endorsed as principles of justice, that endorsement is to be accounted for by an underlying commitment to a view that to treat people who are members as non-members, or people who are wholes as mere parts, is to treat them as less (or more) than they are. The first question to consider, therefore, is whether membership and wholeness are status-affecting attributes, or, at least, whether they may reasonably be regarded as such. If they are, or may reasonably be regarded as such, then the claim that the precepts we have considered are principles of justice will have been shown to be consistent with justice as fittingness. If they may not reasonably be regarded as status-affecting, then either we must claim that although membership or wholeness may not themselves reasonably be regarded as status-affecting, treating in accordance with membership and wholeness is necessary in order to treat in accordance with some attribute which *is* status-affecting, or we must claim that any reasonable endorsement

---

[16] Cf.: 'the theory I shall propose . . . [is offered] as an account of certain distributive principles for the basic structure of society. I assume that any reasonably complete ethical theory must include principles for this fundamental problem and that these principles, whatever they are, constitute its doctrine of justice' (ibid. 10). See also ibid. 5.

of these precepts is not to be viewed as a matter of justice, or we shall have reason to reject justice as fittingness. At all events, a central issue is whether membership and wholeness are status-affecting or, at least, may reasonably be regarded as such. I begin with wholeness.

On what grounds might we consider wholeness to be a status-affecting attribute? There is both an 'internal' and an 'external' aspect to the superior status of wholes. Firstly, though a whole may be composed of parts, those parts must fit together, without fractures or faults, to form an integrated and integral entity, a unity. (The term 'individualism' suggests this integrity, this indivisibility.) To make whole is to make well: 'whole' is etymologically linked to 'heal'. But secondly, the notion of wholeness includes the idea of completeness, of lacking nothing. That which is whole is in an important sense self-sufficient, not dependent (for its identity, say) on another or others. Part of God's status derives from the fact, if it is a fact, that he does not depend on anything outside himself. (The etymology of 'whole' also connects the term to 'holy'.) There is reason, then, to suppose that wholeness is status-affecting. Certainly it seems widely held to be so. That which is whole and complete is generally supposed to be superior to that which is incomplete and a mere part.

What of membership? Is the member superior to the non-member? It is important to be clear what the issue is here. We are concerned with membership *per se*. Membership of a superior group is status-enhancing, but this is so in virtue of the superiority of members of that group, presumably on account of the status-enhancing attributes required for membership of that particular group. But the issue here is whether membership itself is status-enhancing. Are members, *ceteris paribus*, superior to non-members, leaving aside the status associated with what it is that the member is a member of?

We must distinguish membership *per se* from the relation of co-membership. By 'co-membership' I refer to the relation between beings or entities which are members of the same whole. We may note, in passing, the implausibility of the claim that co-membership is status-affecting. There may be some tendency to believe that those who are members of one's own social union—species, race, nation, tribe, community, family—are, *ipso facto*, superior to those who are not, and deserve to be treated as such. But it is hard to see how this view can be made to seem reasonable. This is not, of course, the view that members of a particular family, community, or race (which happens to be our own) are superior in status, and deserve to be treated (by all) as such. This may seem implausible but there is no reason to suppose that it cannot be true. But there is good reason to exclude the claim that members of one's own union are, *ipso facto*, superior: to accept this view would be to accept that status is agent-relative.

This is not to deny the possibility that we ought to treat our co-members differently from others. But it is to deny (if we leave aside the possibility of co-members deserving different treatment on the basis of indirect desert) that such treatment is required *as a matter of justice*. We might, for example, believe that we owe more to our siblings than to people in general, but that we would not act unjustly if we were not to treat our siblings in a special way. Certainly some who are sympathetic to the claims of co-membership have explicitly rejected the idea that such claims are founded on justice.[17]

---

[17] Cf.: 'to some I owe more than justice requires or even permits, not by reason of agreements I have made but instead in virtue of those more or less enduring attachments and commitments which taken together partly define the person I am' (Michael J. Sandel, *Liberalism and the Limits of Justice* (Cambridge, 1982), 179).

If it were indeed the case that, in general, the special treatment of relatives, say, was more than justice permits, it would, for that reason, be a very dubious practice. But it is not clear that this is so. It seems plausible to suppose that, in some circumstances, we may give preferential treatment to our relatives without acting in a manner which treats them as superior, even though it may be that what we do we would need to do in order to treat them as superior. The meaning of our preferential treatment may be that they are simply our relatives, not that they are superior to others. The context in which preference is given colours the meaning of the act. If, for example, the act is one performed in a public capacity where there is assumed to be a duty not to favour relatives (*qua* relatives), a preference may imply a superiority. In a context where no such duty is assumed there may be no such implication. Although we may be unable to claim we are giving equal treatment, we may still be able to claim we are not treating as unequals.

The case for regarding membership as status-affecting seems to be this. The contrast between member and non-member is a contrast between what is a constituent part, what is integral to a whole, and what is at best only peripheral or ancillary. The members of a cast, club, faculty, or team, together constitute the cast, club, faculty, or team. The status of a member *qua* member stems, it seems, from the fact that, in some significant sense, the existence of a greater whole depends on the existence of its members. Thus where the whole derives its status, at least in part, from its depending on nothing (outside itself), membership may be considered status-affecting for the member is depended on (by the whole for its existence).

If we accept that both membership and wholeness are status-affecting, then it follows that partnership is also status-affecting. Partners, to the extent that they are both members and wholes, are both constituent parts of something greater than themselves, and yet complete in themselves; they are both depended on (as members), and independent (as wholes).

Although there is some reason to view both membership and wholeness as status-affecting, the claim that wholeness confers status seems less controversial and more widely shared than the claim that membership does. Thus there are two positions worth considering, and in the remainder of the chapter I want to examine these positions in turn. I consider first the consequences of accepting that both membership and wholeness are, or may reasonably be regarded as, status-affecting; then I look at the consequences of accepting that only wholeness is, or may reasonably be regarded as, status-affecting.

Suppose, then, we were to accept that both membership and wholeness enhance status. What is the relationship between the precepts expressing membership, wholeness, and partnership, and justice as fittingness? If membership, wholeness, and partnership are all status-affecting, then it follows, accepting justice as fittingness, that justice requires that people are treated as members, wholes, or partners, if that is indeed what they are. Now I have claimed that the rationale for a number of distributive precepts is that they are a means of expressing membership, wholeness, or partnership. Thus these precepts represent ways of treating people in accordance with their deserts, albeit indirect deserts. If people are members, wholes, or partners, they deserve to be treated as such, and these precepts are, at least, *a* means by which they may be treated as they deserve.

The precepts we have considered may, therefore, given certain assumptions, be integrated with the view that justice is a member of the fittingness family of concepts. Consider first the precepts associated with exclusive membership. If membership enhances status, then those who are members may be treated unjustly by being treated as a non-member. If, in order to express (exclusive) membership, it is necessary to distribute benefits and burdens according to the interests of the social whole, then to fail to follow this precept will be unjust. If a family is struck by disaster but not all members are expected to contribute so as to mitigate the effects of the disaster, this will be unjust to those not expected to contribute, if it is to treat them as non-members. Women denied the opportunity to contribute to the full extent of their capacities to a war effort may be said to be treated unjustly if they are, thereby, being treated as non-members.[18] This form of argument can also be used to defend a tax system—such as a progressive system—requiring contribution according to ability to pay. Holding each liable to contribute according to ability treats each as a member. A poll tax, by its refusal to impose burdens according to an ability to shoulder them, treats all as non-members. If all are members, this is unjust to all, including those on whom the lightest burdens fall.[19]

---

[18] This is a distinct argument from one grounded on the equal status of women. One may make the argument from failing to treat as a member even if one holds that women are inferior to men. Even a 'junior' member, if treated as a non-member, will be treated unjustly.

[19] This argument against a poll tax, and for the distribution of burdens according to ability, must be distinguished from the argument which highlights the unequal effects of imposing equal burdens on those who are unequally able to shoulder them, and, in particular, focuses on those less

Accepting that wholeness is status-conferring allows us to explain why, if we view people as exclusive wholes, people can deserve in accordance with their contribution. As we noted earlier (2.1), the contribution we make is often affected by factors outside our control. Yet there seems no doubt that many do believe that distribution according to contribution is just, and are unimpressed by the objection that contribution is often a matter of good fortune. And once we view distribution according to contribution as a means of expressing wholeness (by respecting individual fates) we see why this objection is beside the point. The rationale of distribution according to contribution *is* to distribute in accordance with luck, that is, with individual luck. (The defence of distribution according to contribution here parallels that for a poll tax. If the point is to treat each as an exclusive whole, then unequal effects of a poll tax resulting from individual luck are no objection at all.) We may, then, say that people deserve in accordance with their contribution, while accepting both the status requirement, and that contribution need not be status-affecting. The desert basis is wholeness. Thus the apparent counter-example to the status requirement based on contribution noted earlier (2.1) is indeed only apparent.

We may thus explain why it is important not to confuse deserving on the basis of contribution with deserving on the basis of effort. Our willingness to believe that those who make an effort deserve to be rewarded (or, at least, do not deserve not to be rewarded) rests on the presumption that to make an effort is to act rightly. Having a willingness to make an effort is status-enhancing. If we did not believe this were so, if we believed that making an effort were an act of impatience, and that the right action was, say, waiting patiently for

able to contribute and the manner in which they are treated. As we have seen, distributing burdens according to ability may be seen as a parallel to the principle of distributing according to the needs of individuals. The argument for distributing burdens according to ability, grounded on the impact of these burdens on differing individuals' interests, will be available if the union is a partnership, but not if we are concerned with exclusive members. (This argument against a poll tax, like the defence of the principle of need, rests ultimately on treating all as wholes.) So, at least, I have argued.

our desires to be fulfilled, then we would not suppose that
people deserve (to succeed) in accordance with their efforts. If
the basis of deserving in accordance with contribution is
wholeness, then such desert has very different roots. (We can
also see why it is only in the case of effort that we should
speak of *reward*. Where the desert basis is effort what is
deserved can appropriately be described as a reward. But,
assuming that being whole is not something we are responsible for being, the treatment we deserve as wholes we can not
deserve as a reward.)

If we are partners, both members and wholes, we may
explain why it may be thought required as a matter of justice to
distribute in accordance with individual need. As we noted at
the outset (1.1), the compatibility of this precept with justice as
fittingness is by no means clear, for when we fail to treat people
in accordance with their needs it is not obvious that we treat
them as less than they are. Need, it seems, will not function as
a desert basis, for need is not status-affecting (2.4). But given
our account of partnership, and the place of distribution
according to need within it, we may explain how this precept
(understood as GNFC) is a matter of justice, at least between
partners, and how we may, without impropriety, be said to
deserve in accordance with our needs. Distributing according
to need is a means of expressing the membership and wholeness which are the aspects of partnership. Treating according
to need may, then, be reduced to treating according to desert:
we may indirectly deserve in accordance with our needs, the
desert basis being membership and wholeness. Thus the precept of distributing according to need (within partnerships) is
compatible with justice as fittingness.

Finally, I want to suggest that placing compensation within
the context of membership, wholeness, and partnership
allows the precepts of compensation to be brought within the
ambit of justice as fittingness. As we noted earlier (2.1), compensation poses problems both for the account of desert I
have endorsed, and for justice as fittingness. We usually suppose that at least those who suffer through the fault of
another *deserve* compensation; but a person's status is not

generally thought to be affected by suffering through someone else's fault. Suffering through the fault of another cannot, it seems, function as a desert basis, and thus claims that compensation is deserved may seem to violate the status requirement.

As we have seen (2.1), it may be tempting to think that people who suffer through no fault of their own do not deserve to suffer, and thus deserve compensation. But this is fallacious reasoning. We may not deserve to suffer without deserving not to suffer. Nor should deserving to be held liable to compensate be confused with punishing or the expression of censure. Liability to compensate may exist (or is often supposed to exist) even where there is a justification or excuse for doing what was done, and where censure would be inappropriate. If I drive at speed when taking an injured child to hospital and in the process have an accident, then I may deserve not to be censured for my actions, though I may, without injustice, be held liable to compensate those whom I have injured. The justice of compensation is distinct from the justice of reward and punishment.

A basis for the precepts of compensation must, then, be found. Such a basis is provided by analysing desert of compensation, and liability to compensate, as cases of indirect desert, the desert basis being membership or wholeness, or both. In this way the precepts requiring compensation will be shown to be consistent with both the status requirement and justice as fittingness.

If we are exclusive members, and membership confers status, then we may be done an injustice if we are not expected to compensate for the weakness or failing of another member, if we are thereby treated as a non-member. The precept of requiring compensation when and only when someone has acted, or failed to act, and thereby acquired responsibility for the injury of another—the system usually referred to as fault compensation—is to be understood, I have argued, as a system aiming to unravel affairs so as to preserve individual fates, and thereby to treat as whole. If we are exclusive wholes, and wholeness confers status, then justice will require that compensation be provided by, but only by, a person who has so acted, or failed to act. It is as wholes that we deserve such compensation and deserve to be held liable to provide it.[20] If compensation which constitutes a sharing of fates is to be defended as an expression of partnership, it must be argued that such compensation is at least consistent with treating both compensator and compensated as partners, that is, as both members and wholes. A possible desert basis for no-fault compensation, then, is, I am suggesting, partnership.

If, then, we accept that both wholeness and membership are, or may reasonably be thought to be, status-affecting, we will be able to bring within the framework provided by thinking of justice as a fittingness concept various precepts such as distribution according to contribution and need.

I want now to consider the second possibility: that wholeness but not membership is a status-affecting attribute. If we take this view, then we will act unjustly if we fail to treat peo-

---

[20] The fault view might be thought equivalent to the view that those who suffer through no fault of their own deserve compensation, but no one has a duty to provide it (that is, everyone may, without injustice, refuse to provide it) unless the suffering is their fault. To take this view will, presumably, then require a distinction to be drawn between cases where there is a duty to treat people in accordance with their deserts and cases where there is no duty to treat people in accordance with their deserts. I am inclined to think that this way of setting the matter out has nothing to recommend it. It is true that we may say that a person deserves praise without implying that anyone has a duty to provide the praise—there being only a duty not to treat the praise-worthy person as unpraiseworthy. But the case is different with compensation. The holder of the fault view believes it to be not unjust, not only for everyone to fail to offer compensation to the person who suffers through no one's fault, but also for everyone to refuse so to offer. It would seem, then, that what the holder of the fault view believes is that those who suffer through no one's fault do not deserve compensation. There is, it must be admitted, often a reluctance to say as much. This is, presumably, because we so naturally (though fallaciously) infer from 'does not deserve' to 'deserves not'; and, of course, the holder of the fault view need not (and usually will not) hold that those who suffer through no one's fault deserve not to receive compensation. It is, I suggest, this conflation of 'not deserves' with 'deserves not' which leads people to want to say both that those who suffer through no fault of their own deserve compensation, and that everyone may without injustice refuse that compensation. But once we see that the move from 'does not deserve' to 'deserves not' is fallacious, there is no reason to talk as if there is sometimes no duty not to refuse to give that which is deserved.

ple as wholes (assuming they are wholes), but not (*per se*) if we treat people as non-members (even if they are members). I take it that, on this view, if we fail to treat partners as partners we will act unjustly if in so doing we fail to treat them as wholes, but not if we merely fail to treat them as members.

What would be the consequences of such a view? How far are we able to reconcile the precepts we have discussed with conceiving justice as a fittingness concept if only wholeness confers status? Dropping the assumption that membership confers status the position will be the following. If we are properly considered to be wholes, then it is unjust to treat us as mere parts. Thus the precepts associated with treating exclusively as a member will be unjust for following such precepts fails to treat each as whole. Distributing benefits and burdens, and expecting some to compensate for the shortcomings of others, as the interests of the social whole dictate, will be unjust if individuals are wholes and such imposition constitutes treatment as a mere member or part. The precepts associated with treating as exclusively whole will be just (as far as wholeness and membership are concerned) for they are ways of treating as whole, and their denial of membership does not make them unjust. The precepts associated with partnership will also be just (again as far as wholeness and membership are concerned) assuming that these precepts do indeed treat as whole. They also express membership but the fact that they do is not a reason to prefer the precepts of partnership to the precepts of exclusive wholeness as far as justice is concerned. Thus, even if we are partners, we are not treated unjustly if we are treated in accordance with the precepts of exclusive wholeness. We may thereby be treated as other than we are (as non-members when we are members), but not as less than we are.

We may still argue, then, that many of the precepts we have examined are to be understood as precepts of justice because they are means of expressing the wholeness of each. Thus even if we deny that membership confers status, we may still account for such precepts as distribution according to contribution and need within the constraints set by thinking of justice as a fittingness concept. One way to treat as whole may be, as we have seen, to respect individual fates. But respecting individual fates may not be a necessary condition of treating as a whole, and it may be possible to treat people as wholes within the context of treating them also as members. The rationale for a number of distributive precepts may be that they are a means of expressing the wholeness of each individual, for some without, for some within, the context of membership.

It will hardly be surprising if it should turn out that the same status-conferring attribute—wholeness—underlies both the precepts of distribution according to contribution and distribution according to need. It is not implausible to suppose that the belief that each person is a whole is a fundamental tenet of liberalism; and while distribution according to contribution is associated with free-market liberalism, distribution according to need is associated with welfare liberalism. In each case an attempt is being made to give expression to the belief that each person is a whole. The problem of determining a just distribution in a liberal society is, we might say, very much the problem of determining how expression should be given to the wholeness of each person.

What is, perhaps, surprising is that on this view, although the precepts of distribution according to need and distribution according to contribution are precepts of justice (being ways of expressing wholeness), there is reason to say that neither is to be preferred to the other *as a matter of justice.* Assuming both give adequate expression to the wholeness of each, the rival merits of precepts expressing exclusive wholeness and wholeness in partnership respectively are not a matter of justice; and the reason, in a phrase, is that membership is not status-affecting, or is not judged to be so. The issue is, presumably, to be decided by determining whether we are, or can be, exclusively whole or genuine partners, and by arguing that whichever we are, we ought to be treated as such. If we are partners and are treated as exclusively whole, or exclusively whole and are treated as partners, then we are treated as other than we are, but not as less than we are. It is hard to see why in itself there should be thought anything wrong with treating people as other (as against more or less) than they are. In so far as it is wrong, it is wrong presumably because of the consequences of such treatment, say through the loss of a requisite sense of identity.

I conclude, then, that many precepts may be understood as means by which our wholeness as individuals, and our membership of social wholes, may be expressed. Even if we reject the view that membership confers status, we may still argue, providing we accept that wholeness confers status, that such precepts as distribution according to contribution and need may be explicated in terms of indirect desert. Such accounts, I suggest, both expose and illuminate the underlying rationale of these precepts, and show them to be consistent with the claim that justice is a fittingness concept, and that the avoidance of injustice requires only that we treat in accordance with desert. These precepts are not counter-examples to the account of justice I have offered.

4

Promises and Requests

As I have noted (2.4), two important problem cases for justice as fittingness are promises and qualification under some general rule or practice. Both are generally supposed to give rise to entitlements. In this chapter and the next I take up these cases. In the present chapter I discuss the source of the obligation to keep a promise or contract, and its relationship with justice. In the next chapter I take up the problem posed by qualification under a rule.

Much of the present chapter is concerned, then, with the source, or sources, of the obligation to keep a promise. I begin by noting two institution-based accounts. Although I do not wish to reject these accounts as sources of a promissory obligation where the requisite institution exists, I wish to take seriously the view that promises and contracts may give rise to an obligation even where no relevant institution or practice is in operation. One way to try to account for such an obligation (and thereby to solve the problem which promises pose for justice as fittingness) would be to appeal again to the notion of indirect desert, and to argue that all (or most) people possess some status-affecting attribute which we would treat our promisees as lacking if we were to renege on our promises. I examine this possibility briefly, but I do not claim that there is any such attribute. Instead I develop an account of the obligation to keep a promise based on the requirement that we avoid degrading those whom we promise. The function of the argument is to defend justice as fittingness by showing that such an account of justice is not in conflict with a view we may wish to hold, namely that there is reason to act in accordance with a promissory obligation, by virtue of the very nature of the act of promising, such a reason being over and above any reasons we may have deriving from rules or institutions, or, indeed, from any utilitarian considerations.

Promissory acts are—at least in modern Western culture—the means *par excellence* by which obligations are created. It is not surprising, then, that promising has received from philosophers the attention it has. But there is no reason to assume that promissory acts are the sole means by which obligations can be generated; and in the latter part of the chapter I argue that a request may generate an obligation, and in much the same way as a promise. I also suggest that this argument may provide a solution to the problem of political obligation, thereby enabling us to avoid the problems associated with the traditional social contract approach.

4.1 *The Obligation to Keep a Promise*

Promises pose a problem for the account of justice I have given for it may seem that, by failing to keep our promises, we act unjustly towards those whom we promise, but without treating them as less than they are, as lacking any status-affecting attribute which in fact they possess. It seems, then, that by failing to honour a promise we do not deny anyone what they deserve. Certainly we do not usually suppose that we enhance the status of those whom we promise by making a promise to them.

Let us set aside considerations of simple comparative justice. If I keep my promises to only some people, I may be said to be treating unjustly those to whom I do not keep faith; I may be said to be treating them as of less account as compared to those with whom I do keep faith. This may well be true. But it will remain to be explained what reason I act contrary to if I keep my promises to no one. It is this question I want to consider.

One account of the obligation to keep a promise derives the obligation from the principle of fairness.[1] In making a

[1] John Rawls, *A Theory of Justice* (Oxford, 1972), 344–50.

promise we take advantage of a useful social practice, but in reneging we fail to do our share to maintain that practice. We act as a parasite. If this argument is sound, then reneging is unjust, assuming, as seems reasonable, that violating the principle of fairness is unjust. Now I have argued earlier (1.5) that the injustice of violating the principle of fairness rests on the requirement to treat equals as equals. Thus, if that argument was sound, this explanation of the injustice of failing to keep a promise follows the pattern which justice as fittingness requires.

We may also argue that failing to keep a promise is a simple institutional injustice. We may, that is, argue that there is an established (and not unjust) rule that promises be kept, and that to renege on one's promises is to deny people that to which they are entitled under that rule, and therefore unjust. On this view, then, whatever account we offer for the injustice of ignoring entitlements (providing, of course, that it does not rely, in its turn, on a claim that reneging on a promise is unjust) will explain why failing to keep a promise is unjust. If we take this view, we will regard the argument of the present chapter as superfluous: the argument of the next chapter will be sufficient to deal with all entitlements, including those deriving from promises.

Now there is much to be said for these arguments from institutions as regards giving us reasons to keep our promises. Nevertheless, there is reason not to rely exclusively on them. Firstly, the argument from fairness does not, on the face of it, explain why to fail to keep a promise is to wrong the promisee. We act unjustly because we treat ourselves as more than a mere equal; and we wrong all others in so far as we treat them as less than ourselves. But if we explain the wrongness of reneging by pointing to a failure to do our share to maintain a practice, we do not explain why the promisee is wronged in a way in which third parties to our promises are not. Secondly, both arguments rely on the existence of a practice of promise-keeping, and thus neither is able to explain why there should be such a practice. Now to be sure a promise-keeping convention is socially useful, and its existence is certainly not puzzling. But it is tempting to think that the convention of keeping promises is not merely socially useful. Many are inclined to the view that keeping faith is the right thing to do in itself, and that this is a reason to have the convention. On this view, then, we have reason to have a convention that promises be kept, even if it is also true that *a* reason (or *some* reasons) to keep our promises derive only from the existence of that convention.

I want to take seriously the view that we have reason to keep the promises we make independently of the existence of any convention. But if this is so, then the problem posed by promises for the account of justice I have given is not avoided by an appeal to the principle of fairness or institutional justice. It is, therefore, safest to assume that the problem is not solved by these arguments.

Suppose, then, that we set aside any appeal to institutions and conventions. How are we to explain why we ought to keep the promises we make? Why do we act wrongly if we renege? Let us also set aside the utilitarian reasons we often have for keeping our promises. Such reasons will be contingent on the consequences of reneging and will very likely not always apply. What we want to know is whether there is reason to keep a promise *per se*, a reason which arises from the very nature of the promising act itself.

One non-contingent reason to keep a promise is this. To renege on one's promises (without an appropriate reason, at least) is to make oneself less worthy of trust. It is, therefore, to undermine one's trustworthiness, and thus to degrade oneself if, as most of us believe, trustworthiness is a virtue. One reason to keep a promise, therefore, is the avoidance of self-degradation: the avoidance of making oneself less or lower than one would otherwise have been.[2]

---

[2] Trustworthiness is, presumably, a disposition, and if this is so, it needs to be shown how it is that an act of betrayal increases, rather than merely signals, our untrustworthiness. There are a number of possible accounts which might be developed. We might argue that an act of betrayal makes other such acts more likely in the future, say by undermining the habit of loyalty; or that at least here the distinction between the way we are, and the way others perceive us to be, collapses; or deny that our actions are merely

But if we are to argue that we should keep our promises in order to avoid the degradation of becoming untrustworthy, then we will need to be assured that the fact that trustworthiness is a virtue does not depend on the rightness of promise-keeping. Without some independent explanation of why trustworthiness is a virtue the argument will have a trivial circularity. But an independent argument may be available. We may argue that trustworthiness, and such related notions as dependability, reliability, faithfulness, and integrity, have, as their central image, the notion of solidity, of an entity of definite shape and significant density, unchanging over time. These are the characteristics possessed by, say, a rock or a brick and lacked by a cloud.[3] People are dependable if they are supportive, if we can hang from them, as the etymology of 'dependable' (a relative of 'suspend' and 'pendulum') suggests. A dependable person does not let others down; a person of integrity does not disintegrate, fall apart, when relied upon. These various notions, then, make use of the metaphor of a solid physical object. A closely related virtue is constancy—of not being capricious or fickle—for only if one has constancy can one be trusted, relied upon, over time. Solidity and continuity, then, are readily associated.

Identifying the central metaphor at work helps to explain why trustworthiness is a virtue. To be sure, what is solid and stable over time may be useful for achieving many and various purposes. But perhaps trustworthiness is not merely useful—perhaps it is a virtue at least in part because of its contribution to a less questionable identity and reality: what is solid, what is substantial, seems more real.[4] As we move

signals of character and dispositions, and argue that actions are, at least in part, constitutive of character. It is, we might say, a part of what it is to have free will that our character and dispositions are not simply given and determining: a disposition to betray does not preclude choosing not to betray. We are, then, continuously generating our characters by our actions.

[3] Thus the appropriateness of the term 'brick' for a reliable person, and of Christ's reference to Peter as a rock on which to build his church (Matthew 16: 18).

[4] Cf.: 'Socrates, Buddha, Moses, Gandhi, Jesus—these figures capture our imagination and attention by their greater reality. They are more vivid, concentrated, focused, delineated, integrated, inwardly beautiful. Compared to

around, such objects impede us, offer resistance. The reality of that which is airy, nebulous, insubstantial, liable to disintegrate is more open to question. In addition, if one part of what exists is solid, well-integrated, and enclosed within a definite boundary, then it will be hard not to regard such a part of what there is as a separate, individual entity. The virtue of constancy can also be understood in terms of identity and reality. That which exists unchanging over time has—or seems to have—a greater claim to be regarded as an entity. A person who is constantly changing their commitments, beliefs, allegiances can be likened to a series of ephemera; such a person is not a firm point of reference in a changing world, is not a person of substance. And, of course, degree of reality is widely viewed as status-affecting.[5] If this were not so, there would have been no ontological argument for the existence of God.

There is reason, then, to accept trustworthiness and related notions as virtues, and without this claim needing to rely on the rightness of promise-keeping. Nevertheless, there is good reason not to rely on the argument from self-degradation: as with the argument from fairness, it is not clear that this argument can explain why, when we renege, we wrong our promisee. Thus although the avoidance of self-degradation may provide *a* reason to keep a promise, it seems not to provide an explanation of why promises *qua* promises obligate; indeed this reason for action applies as readily to vows we might make to ourselves.

How are we to explain why reneging on a promise wrongs the promisee? There are at least two ways in which we may wrong people, corresponding to the two types of reason for

us, they are more real' (Robert Nozick, *The Examined Life* (New York, 1989), 131).

[5] Cf.: 'what is more real is somehow better' (ibid. 139). Lawrence uses our acceptance of this point in his comparison of the bourgeoisie with mushrooms: his reference to the bourgeoisie as 'appearances' not only suggests their hypocrisy, but also their fleeting insubstantial character; by questioning their reality Lawrence pours scorn on them. (D. H. Lawrence, 'How Beastly the Bourgeois Is', in *Selected Poems* (Harmondsworth, 1950), 137–8).

action noted earlier (1.2). We may wrong by treating unfittingly, by treating people as less than they are; and we may wrong by degrading, by making people less than they might otherwise have been. Thus if we can explain how it is that to break a promise is to treat the promisee unfittingly, or to degrade the promisee, or both, we shall have an account of why reneging on a promise wrongs the promisee.

Consider first whether to renege on our promises is to treat our promisees unfittingly, as less than they are. As we noted earlier, to be promised is not thereby to have one's status enhanced: we do not become more worthy of esteem by being promised. Nevertheless, arguments relying on the notion of indirect desert are still possible: perhaps people possess some status-affecting attribute such that to renege on a promise is to treat them as lacking that attribute.

Should we say that a person who reneges on their promises treats their promisees as if they do not matter, as beings who do not have a good of their own? This account is unsatisfactory. We may agree that, as a matter of contingent fact, people who renege on their promises often do view those whom they have promised as not mattering. But this is simply a consequence of the fact that the normal explanation of why people renege on promises is that they give way to self-interest. And people who are too ready to act in their own interests do indeed treat others without sufficient regard.

But this is (at best) no more than an explanation of why we must give due concern to the interests of others, and attach due weight to those reasons for action which relate to others. It does not explain why by promising we give ourselves a reason to act which we would not otherwise have, a reason to which we may fail to give due regard when we renege. We can see this if we consider a case of reneging on a promise not out of self-interest, but out of a concern for the interests of the promisee. Suppose I come to the view that it would be contrary to my promisee's interests for me to keep my promise, though my promisee disagrees with this assessment, and is unwilling to release me from the promise. To avoid the problems generated by the paternalism involved we may suppose the promisee is a child, and that any paternalism is appropriate.

Now in deciding whether to keep my promise I face a genuine dilemma, and how I ought to act depends, it seems plausible to say, on the extent to which keeping the promise is contrary to my promisee's interests. That is, there is a clash between two reasons for action. But if the reason to keep the promise were simply to avoid treating the promisee as a person who does not matter, that reason will disappear in a case such as this; for there can be no suggestion that by not keeping my promise I am treating the promisee as a person who does not matter. Thus if that were the reason to keep the promise, there would be no dilemma; and if we accept that there is a genuine dilemma here, we must reject this account of the reason to keep a promise.

I conclude, then, that the reason to keep a promise is not simply to ensure that we avoid treating people as if they do not matter. The explanation has to be much more closely related to the nature of promising than that.[6] An argument which does attempt to focus more closely on the nature of promising makes use of the distinction we draw between those who are capable of being promised and those who are not. For although a person's status is not enhanced by being promised, it is plausible to suppose that a being able to be promised is superior to one which is not. To make a promise is to invite trust or faith, but only certain beings can trust and have faith. A machine, for example, cannot trust. If a capacity to trust requires rationality and free will, then it is plausible to suppose that the capacity to trust is associated with enhanced status. But we need pursue this issue no further for it is, surely, implausible to suppose that by failing to keep our promises we treat our promisee as a being unable to be promised. *Ex hypothesi*, the promisor has already made the promise, thereby treating the promisee as able to be promised. This is

---

[6] There are, no doubt, other objections to this account. It is unclear, for example, on the account proposed why we should have more reason to act in accordance with a promise than with a statement of intent we have made, where this has been relied upon.

sufficient to block any possibility of reneging constituting treatment of the promisee as unable to be promised.

I shall not argue that the obligation to keep a promise can be explained by appeal to indirect desert. I do not claim that such a reduction cannot be achieved, though I do not see how it can be done. Certainly any attempted reduction must take seriously the fact that—as the term 'obligation' suggests—the promisor is bound to the promisee in a way in which no one else is: promises in themselves generate a reason for action for the promisor which no one else has. The account of the obligation which I will now develop does attempt to take this binding seriously. But it is not an argument which shows that by reneging we treat our promisee unfittingly; it is an argument to show that reneging degrades.

Suppose I promise to mark my students' essays by a particular date, and then fail to do so. And suppose my students believed, on the basis of my promise, that I would mark the essays by the date I gave. By reneging on my promise I make one of my students' beliefs false. Have I, thereby, degraded my students? It may seem not. Many reasonable beliefs turn out to be false, and it is no discredit, we might argue, to have held a reasonable, though false, belief. But although holding a false belief may not be a failing, it is widely admitted to be a failing to adopt beliefs too readily, as when our beliefs are not warranted by the evidence available. To go beyond the evidence in our beliefs is a form of foolishness: it is this failing we exhibit when we make the mistake of thinking we know more than we do. Wisdom requires us to acknowledge when we do not know, and to adjust our beliefs accordingly.

Now a promise invites the promisee to form a belief on the basis of the word of the promisor. The promisee is invited to believe that the promisor will act as promised—at least unless certain conditions obtain. At the very least the promisee is invited to believe that the promisor will treat the fact of promising as providing a significant reason to act in accordance with the promise. But the word of the promisor is not to be taken as mere evidence that the action will follow as promised. Promises invite trust, and to trust is to go beyond the evidence. To treat a promise as mere evidence is not to trust.

Why must a promise be taken as more than evidence if the promisor is to have been trusted? Consider again the students whose essays I have promised to mark. How should they allow my promise to affect their beliefs? One way is to treat my promise as no more than evidence. Now if the students are to treat my undertaking as evidence, they will need to determine how good a piece of evidence it is. It would be reasonable for them to try to establish with what frequency such undertakings are kept by people like me. How often, they might ask, do lecturers with similar characteristics to me, similar age, experience, class, upbringing, psychological type, and so on, keep such promises? Suppose, following such an inquiry, and making allowance for any further information they may have, their best estimate turns out to be 23 per cent. It will be rational for them to believe that there is a 23 per cent chance of my keeping my promise. To believe there is a higher probability would be to go beyond the evidence.

Now to view my undertaking in this way, and to adopt the degree of belief appropriate to the evidence, involves no trust. (Nor can trust be simply added on: when we trust, it is not that we make the inquiries and then add on something for the trust, say another 10 per cent.) To trust, or to have faith, is to view a promise as a commitment, not merely as evidence of a possible future action. To the extent that we trust, we are firm in conviction, free from doubt and uncertainty. To the extent that we doubt, we do not trust. But our belief cannot be an expression of trust where we have proof or sufficient evidence for our degree of belief, and are aware that we do. Puzzling as it may seem, then, when we trust we must be free from doubt, but free from doubt in the face of uncertainty.

It is important not to mistake genuine trust for impostors. It is sometimes rational to behave as if we are sure when we are not. To achieve some ends, it may help to act as if we have beliefs we do not have. It may help to pull off a deal if I act with confidence in my associates. It may be rational to act as if we trust when we do not. But such behaviour is not to be confused with genuine trust: it is to pretend to trust when we do not have the firm belief which trusting requires. Indeed, this process may operate at a deeper level: it may be pragmatically rational not only to act as if we trust when we do not, but to try, as far as we are able, to acquire the firm belief which trust requires. If I am able to acquire such a belief I may avoid, or at least reduce, the risk of inadvertently betraying my doubts.

But manufactured trust is a devalued coin, and there are limits to the functions which such trust—if indeed it is properly called trust—can perform. Manufactured trust may help us to achieve an optimal outcome in a game. But to manufacture trust is to trust for reasons external to the practice of trusting itself. It is to be willing to give trust to the untrustworthy as well as the trustworthy, and it cannot, therefore, express a belief that a person is worthy of trust. (The trust of a person who has taken trust-inducing pills pays us no respect.) Although, as we have seen, to trust is to adopt beliefs to a degree which goes beyond our evidence for them, an act of trust must be the act of a free and rational agent, if it is to perform the central role in interpersonal relations of affirming trustworthiness. To manufacture trust is to undermine one's epistemic rationality in the sense required for one's trust to be affirming of trustworthiness.

Though to trust is always to go beyond the evidence, the decision whether to trust or not can be made on the basis of evidence. Trust may be more or less grounded, more or less reasonable. It is reasonable when we have evidence, often based on past behaviour, to support a belief that a person is worthy of trust. Trust is blind when it is based on no such evidence, and courageous, perhaps foolhardy, when given in the face of known contrary evidence. Those who are willing to trust without evidence of trustworthiness are more easily deceived, more gullible.

Now to trust is to place oneself at risk—at risk of being duped, of being made a fool of. It is part of the nature of trust that it carries such a risk. If trust is required, and is not unreasonable on the evidence available, one may defend oneself against a charge of gullibility if one's trust is betrayed. Nevertheless, one has still been duped. One can rebut a charge of having been duped only by claiming that one did not really believe, that is, by denying that one really did trust. And though the stigma attaching to being duped may be less than that attaching to being shown gullible, such a stigma, for many, at least, still exists.[7] It exists, I suggest, because of the questionable compatibility of trust and (epistemic) rationality, and the status accorded to rationality. That such a stigma should attach to those who are duped, but who are not thereby shown to have been gullible, will be denied by those who reject the possibility of moral luck; for whether we turn out to be a dupe, made a fool, will depend on the actions of those whose promises we accept. Once we have given our trust we are at their mercy. Those who deny the possibility of moral luck will, then, deny that whether we are made dupes of is something by which we can be appraised or assessed. But it is, to say the least, by no means clear that moral luck does not exist, and hence it is not clear that we are wrong to feel degraded when we are let down, no matter how reasonable our trust was. It would seem, then, that the only way to avoid the risk of degradation is never to trust. But, as we shall see shortly, such a strategy carries (moral) risks of its own.

The argument, then, is that we have reason to keep our promises because reneging makes fools of those to whom we promise. The argument presupposes that wisdom is a virtue, and that to become a fool is to be degraded. I shall assume that these claims are granted. But it remains to be explained why it is the promisor who is responsible for the promisee's becoming a fool. It is, after all, the promisee who decides whether to trust or not. Why, then, should responsibility for the degradation of the promisee be laid at the door of the promisor?

Is it that, by promising, the promisor leads the promisee to hold the false belief, and is therefore responsible for it? The promisor leads the promisee to hold the belief, we might say,

---

[7] As Trollope puts it: 'the part of a dupe is never dignified' (Anthony Trollope, *Barchester Towers*, vol. i, ch. 15).

since if the promisor had not promised, the false belief would not have been held. But there are many ways in which one person may lead another to hold beliefs; and not all of these ways have the effect of relieving the holder of a false belief of responsibility for that belief. We may lead others to beliefs, including beliefs about our future actions, not only by promising, but by predicting and by making statements of intent. Why is it, then, that you are responsible for my false belief if you make a promise to me, but not—or, at least, to nothing like the same extent—if you merely predict what you will do, or tell me what you intend to do?

We may explain why the degradation of the promisee is the responsibility of the promisor, why promisees are *made* fools of, rather than make fools of themselves, by contrasting promises with statements of intent. It is important to distinguish between promising and indicating an intention. It may not always be clear whether we have promised or merely indicated an intention, given the ambiguity of the phrases we often use to make promises. Nevertheless, it is clear that to promise is not simply to make a statement of intent: I can perfectly well state my intention to mark an essay by a particular date, but decline to promise. Or applicants for student loans may be required to declare that they intend to reside permanently in a country, but not required to undertake to do so.

There are two stages in reasoning from a statement of intent to a belief about future action. Firstly, it is necessary to decide whether to believe that the statement is true, that is, whether the person really has the intention claimed. Secondly, it is necessary to decide whether, if the person does have the intention claimed, future actions will accord with present intentions. Trust may feature in the first stage of this process. If I believe firmly, on the basis of your statement, that you have the intention you have indicated, then I am trusting your word. If you successfully lie about your intentions, you will dupe me. But if your statement of intent is honest, you will not dupe me, even if you change your mind, or are unable to act as you intended. If I firmly believe, on the basis of your statement of intent, that you will act as you have indicated, then my belief will turn out to be false if you do not so act. But I shall not have been made a fool of, though I may have exposed my own foolishness.

Why is it that you are responsible for my unwarranted false belief if you promise, but not if you merely indicate (honestly) an intention? I suggest that the explanation is this: if you make a promise to me, I have to decide whether to trust you or not. If I do trust you, then I may end up being duped. But if I do not trust you, I risk doing you an injustice. I believe you to be less than trustworthy, which, if you are trustworthy, is unjust: I treat you as less than you are. A promisee thus faces a dilemma. But if you have only indicated an intention, I face no such dilemma. If I do not believe firmly that you will act as you have said you intend to act, then I do you no injustice, even if you do so act. (At least, this is true if changing one's mind is not a moral failing. My belief that you may change your mind, even if mistaken, will not be unjust, just as a belief that you have red hair, even if mistaken, is not unjust.)

Now it is this risk of injustice (injustice by the promisee, not the promisor) which is crucial. It is this risk which absolves the promisee from responsibility for becoming a fool when trust is given and the promise is not kept. For to avoid the possibility of doing an injustice, it is morally necessary for the promisee to believe firmly that the promise will be kept.[8] Given this necessity, responsibility for the false belief is transmitted to the promisor. It is the promisor who is responsible, and we may rightly say that the promisor makes a fool of the promisee. But where there is only a statement of intent, it is the believer who is responsible for any unwarranted false belief, for the believer is not required, on pain of doing an injustice, to hold an unwarranted belief. (Assuming, of course, that the statement of intent was honest. If you have deceived me, then you are responsible for my false belief: I had

---

[8] Cf.: 'Aristotle indeed made a little noted observation that one sense of "necessary" is: "that without which some good will not be attained or some evil avoided" ' (G. E. M. Anscombe, *The Collected Papers of G. E. M. Anscombe, iii: Ethics, Religion and Politics* (Oxford, 1981), 100). See also pp. 18–19.

to trust that your statement was honest, on pain of doing you the injustice of thinking you dishonest when you are not.)

Do any qualifications need to be added to this account? I want to mention two. Firstly, we can be duped only if we trust. Hence the obligation to keep a promise in order to avoid duping one's promisee applies only where the promisee has, or may have, come to trust, thereby relying upon the promise. Thus we might say that, in so far as the obligation is thought to arise in the manner I have described, it is reliance which generates the obligation to keep a promise. But if we speak of the necessity of reliance to generate the obligation, it is important to be clear what counts as reliance.

Suppose I make a promise, and my promisee, confident that I will not keep my word, arranges her affairs so that her interests will be seriously harmed when I renege. (Perhaps she is confident of successfully suing me for breach of promise, and relishes teaching me a lesson for my anticipated betrayal.) In such a case, though my promisee is acting in such a way as to place (some of) her interests at risk with respect to my promise, and may later claim to have suffered as a result of having relied upon the promise, she has not relied upon the promise in the sense which the argument I have given requires. She is not made a fool of when I do not keep the promise. (Indeed it may be that only by breaking my promise can I prevent my promisee from making a fool of herself.)

Trust, then, is necessary for the reliance which is required. But trust is also sufficient. It is not necessary for the promisee's interests to be at stake. We do not avoid wronging someone simply because our actions do not harm their interests. Of course material reliance is normally a relatively unambiguous expression of trust, and hence an unwillingness to place one's interests at risk with respect to a promise may suggest a lack of trust. Nevertheless, trust *per se* places the promisee at risk. Relief at a fortunate escape, together with the knowledge gained from the experience, may make the diminution easier to bear; but if we have indeed given our trust, we are diminished by betrayal.

A second qualification may need to be added, depending on

the view we take of the relationship between trustworthiness and possible failings. On one view complete and total trustworthiness is a virtue; no one can be condemned for being too trustworthy. A different view is to see the virtue of trustworthiness as a mean between two failings: untrustworthiness on the one hand, and a rigid, inflexible fastidiousness on the other. If we take this view, then it *is* possible for a person to be condemned for being too trustworthy, too reliable.

Now if trustworthiness is a mean, then it is possible, in principle at least, that promises do not always create obligations in the way I have described. According to the argument I have given, I have reason to keep a promise because if I do not, I may dupe my promisee. But I dupe her only if I am responsible for her (unwarranted) false belief. And I am responsible only because she, on pain of doing me an injustice, must hold the belief that I will act as I have promised. But the injustice arises only if trustworthiness to the degree required is indeed a virtue. If it is not, and particularly if it is a fault, this argument unravels.

To illustrate: suppose I take a book from your office, leaving you a note in which I promise to return it to you the following week. I subsequently discover that you will be spending next week on an island so remote that the only way of returning the book to you is to hire an aircraft, fly over the island, and parachute it down to you, all at great expense. Now we might argue that to claim I have made a promise to return the book to you no matter where you are is to ignore implicit background assumptions, and so we might deny the existence of any obligation. But let us assume for the sake of argument that what I have done does constitute promising to return the book to you on the island. Does it follow that I have an obligation to go to the trouble and expense of returning the book, arising from the risk of duping you if I do not attempt to do so? If trustworthiness is a mean, perhaps not.

Suppose I do hire the aircraft and return the book to you. Would this be an action exhibiting exemplary trustworthiness, and thus worthy of admiration, or would it be the act of a person fastidious to a fault? If trustworthiness of the degree required is not a virtue, then it follows that you are not required, on pain of doing me an injustice, to believe that I will parachute the book down to you. (If you believe that I will not thus return the book, and I do, then your belief about me is false, but it is not unjust.) And if you are not required to believe that I will return the book, then I am not responsible for your false belief if you believe I will return the book and I do not. And thus I have no obligation to keep the promise arising from my duty not to dupe you. If, then, we take the view that one can be fastidious to a fault, inflexible, rigid, and hence too reliable, then we must concede that a promise which only such a person could be expected to keep may not give rise to an obligation in the way I have described.

I conclude that a promisor has reason to keep a promise, arising from the duty not to degrade (and in particular from the duty not to dupe), at least where the promise is accepted, and where the promise is not of such a nature that to keep the promise would be to exhibit trustworthiness to a degree that is no longer a virtue. I emphasize that the argument is intended to show how an obligation to keep a promise can arise. I do not claim that such an obligation cannot be accounted for in other ways. (Hence I do not claim that we have no obligation, still less no reason, to keep promises made to untrusting promisees.) But I do claim that since we have this reason for action we do indeed have an obligation to keep our promises. The account also explains why it is so appropriate to speak of obligation in such a case: the moral fates of the parties are bound together.

The argument does not, however, show that the reneging promisor treats the promisee *unjustly*. I have not argued that we must keep our promises to avoid *treating* our promisees as fools (when they are not); the argument shows that we must not renege if we are to avoid *making* a fool of our promisee. The objection to breaking faith is not that it is unjust, but that it degrades. What, then, are the implications of the argument for justice as fittingness?

The function of the argument I have given is to allay, at least to some degree, a doubt about the account of justice I am defending. The doubt arises in the following way. Suppose we believe that promises create obligations, not simply by virtue of there being an established practice that promises ought to be kept, but because, we believe, we have a reason to keep our promises independent of the existence of the practice. Now if this is our view, we may wonder if this reason—whatever it is—is compatible with viewing justice as a fittingness concept. I have argued that there is indeed a reason to act which arises out of the very nature of a promise, but that this reason is not one such that contrary action is unjust. Of course I have not shown that there is not some other reason arising out of the nature of a promise, a reason of which it *is* true that contrary action is unjust. By its nature, it is not easy to see how one could show that there is no such reason.[9] But to the extent that we are led to suspect that there may be such a reason by a belief that promises, by their nature, obligate (independently of the existence of established practices), the argument I have given undercuts this suspicion—by showing how we can explain how promises obligate but in a way which is grounded on the avoidance of degradation rather than injustice.

---

[9] That there is such a reason is denied by Feinberg: 'Not all cases of wrongful promise-breaking are instances of injustice of any kind (*pace* Hobbes)' (Joel Feinberg, *Rights, Justice, and the Bounds of Liberty* (Princeton, 1980), 269). It may seem odd to claim that, as far as non-institution-based reasons for action are concerned, reneging on a promise is wrong but not unjust. Certainly many theorists have claimed that failing to keep a promise is unjust. As noted by Feinberg, these include Hobbes, who goes as far as to suggest that *only* promise-breaking is unjust: 'the definition of INJUSTICE, is no other than *the not Performance of Covenant*. And whatsoever is not Unjust, is *Just*' (Thomas Hobbes, *Leviathan*, ch. 15). According to Mill, one of the 'modes of action . . . which are classed, by universal or widely spread opinion . . . as Unjust' includes 'to *break faith* with anyone' (J. S. Mill, *Utilitarianism*, ch. 5 (in *Utilitarianism*, ed. Mary Warnock (London, 1962), 298–9). But this is very doubtful, at least if normal English usage is any guide. Although it is agreed that, other things being equal at least, it is wrong to renege when one has given one's word, it is striking that those who do not keep their promises are rarely castigated as unjust.

4.2 *The Obligation to Meet a Request*

As I suggested earlier, promises are probably the least controversial means by which we may generate an obligation. But it does not follow that they are the only means, and I now wish to argue that requests may also generate obligations. Of course it is widely supposed that a request does not create any obligation to comply.[10] Nevertheless, that view is not universal.[11]

I shall assume that to have an obligation is to have a reason for action, and that this reason arises from some previous committing action—often, though not necessarily, an action

---

[10] Cf.: 'As I drive up to London in my comfortable car, you may feel and tell me that (out of beneficence) I ought to stop and give a lift to the inoffensive-looking person standing hopefully, thumb suitably protruded, at the side of the road; and I might agree with that; but I would not, I think, agree that I have, or am under, an *obligation* to do so. . . . I am not *bound*, as the driver of a private car, to offer lifts to everyone, or even to anyone, who may solicit that service' (Geoffrey Warnock, *The Object of Morality* (London, 1971), 94).

[11] Cf.: 'obligations . . . are typically incurred by previous committing actions. . . . what actions are committal will vary from society to society. To us, the most familiar committing actions are promising or giving one's word generally . . . less clearly delineated cases of obligations, at least in our society, [include] . . . the obligation to give money to a beggar having been asked for it. This . . . case illustrates a concept which has relatively rare application for us—that of being put under an obligation to someone by their conduct rather than one's own. In certain societies, I believe, a knock on the door of one's house by a stranger at once puts one under an obligation of a firm kind to provide hospitality and, if necessary, a bed for the night' (E. J. Lemmon, 'Moral Dilemmas', *Philosophical Review*, 71 (1962), 141).

Lemmon's claim that 'what actions are committal will vary from one society to another' suggests that obligations may depend on prior institutional structures. This may be so, and I do not wish to deny the possibility of institutionally based obligations. Of course, where there is no relevant institution, there can be no institutionally based obligation; and if in 'our society' there is no general convention of being put under an obligation by a request, there can be, for us, no institutionally based obligation to comply with a request. But the fact that there would have been an obligation, if the requisite institution had existed, does not imply that there can be no obligation in the absence of such an institution. The possibility of a pre-institutional obligation remains. And it is for the existence of such an obligation—a *pre*-institutional obligation to comply with a request—that I want to argue.

of the person who becomes obliged. (In so far as we may distinguish obligations from duties it is the existence of this previous committing action which, at least in part, enables us to do so.) It is a mistake, I shall assume, to suppose that it is part of the very nature of an obligation that it is created by the voluntary act of the person who acquires the obligation. If the point is not conceded, we may speak of quasi-obligations, which are just like normal obligations except that others may impose them. But it seems preferable not to limit our use of 'obligation' in this way. Further, although obligations are often thought to be particularly pressing, and the reasons for action which underlie them particularly strong, I shall not assume that it is this which characterizes an obligation. That is, I assume that what is distinctive about an obligation is the *kind* of reason for action whose existence is signalled by the existence of the obligation, not the *strength* of that reason.

The form of my argument that requests generate obligations is comparative: I argue that there is reason to act in accordance with some requests (a reason generated by the very act of requesting) in much the same way as there is reason to act in accordance with a promise. Thus if it is appropriate to speak of an obligation in the case of the one, it is also appropriate in the case of the other.

But to begin we need an account of what a request is. To request is to perform a speech act of a particular type.[12] A request is not a report or statement; like a promise, it is neither true nor false. But just as promising is closely related to expressing an intention, so requesting is closely related to expressing a wish. (Our promises are sincere only if we intend to honour them; our requests are sincere only if we wish to see them met.) It is true that, just as we often make promises by locutions which can also be statements of intent, we often make requests by use of expressions which may merely state wishes. But just as we can make a statement of intent without promising, so we may state our wishes without requesting. To

---

[12] My account of requesting follows closely that of John R. Searle: see *Speech Acts* (London, 1969), esp. 64–71.

request is to do something in addition to expressing our wishes.

What is this additional something? A request, when used normally and seriously, is an attempt to get the requestee to act in a particular way.[13] Not any such attempt is a request. Requesting can be contrasted with other ways of attempting to affect the actions of others, such as ordering and commanding, suggesting and advising, and making threats and offers. To request is to attempt to affect the actions of another person, but not by compulsion; the attempt is made by an appeal to the reason of the requestee.

Is this appeal made by drawing the attention of the requestee to a reason to act which already exists, or by providing an additional reason to act, a reason which would not have existed had the request not been made? We should reject the view that a request does no more than draw attention to a reason to act which the requestee already has. That would leave unclear what the point of requesting is, as against merely stating our wishes. It is true, of course, that we often have, independently of a request, reason to do what we are requested to do. To act in accordance with a sincere request is to act in accordance with the requestor's wishes, and such action can often be expected to increase that requestor's happiness or welfare. And if, as seems reasonable, we have reason to increase happiness where we can, we shall often have reason to act in accordance with others' wishes. Certainly a request may draw our attention to such a reason, and it may provide information we require if we are to know how we should act. But it is not necessary for attention to be drawn, or information given, *by the making of a request*. It is enough to achieve this end simply to state that the wish exists. If we were to believe that requests do no more than refer to existing reasons, we should be unable to see the point of a request, as against the mere expression of a wish. (Nor can the point of making a request be to deny that there is a reason not to act

---

[13] Searle refers to this as the 'essential condition' (ibid. 66). 'Normally and seriously' here excludes such uses as telling jokes, acting in a play, teaching a language, and so on. See ibid. 57.

in accordance with the wish. Certainly a request implies that compliance will not be resented as an invasion. But it goes beyond doing so: to make a request is not merely to invite or permit.) I conclude that requests are attempts to affect the actions of others, and the attempt is made by providing a reason to act which the requestee would not otherwise have. Requests, by their nature, must be supposed to generate reasons for action.

In passing we may note that this argument, if successful, may provide an explanation of the point of prayer to an omniscient being. It may be thought that, if God is already aware of what we wish, prayer can serve no objective purpose. (It may be allowed, of course, that prayer can serve subjective purposes.) If my argument is sound, this view is mistaken: our prayers can give even an omniscient God a reason to act which he would not otherwise have.

As we have seen, to request is to attempt to get someone to act in accordance with our wishes. But it is not to offer anything in return, nor is it to threaten anything if the request is ignored. Nor, when we request, do we claim a right to determine our requestee's action. And yet, despite all this, we are to regard a request as an attempt to affect action. To request is to attempt to affect another's actions, by doing no more than presenting those wishes in a form which constitutes an attempt to affect action. But if that is what requesting is, it follows that to make a request of someone is to treat the requestee as someone for whom our wishes, in themselves, can provide a reason for action. To request is to treat the requestee as such a person, as a person who is not cold, uncaring, indifferent, unloving, disregardful.

It is sometimes suggested that we view ourselves as complete and closed systems, in the sense that the wishes of any particular individual are viewed as exclusively and exhaustively related to that individual's actions. We act rationally, on this view, when we act on the basis of all and only our own wishes, acting in such a way as is likely to maximize their satisfaction. But such a view is incompatible with responding to a request as a request. If we really do conceive ourselves entirely in this way, then the point of requesting will be lost to us. (Indeed if we take this view, we may be unable to see a request as anything more than the rather pushy expression of a wish.) After all, on this account *your* wish simply cannot, in itself, provide a reason for *me* to act. How could you suppose, therefore, that you were attempting to get me to act simply by presenting your wishes to me? To suppose that our requests are attempts to affect the actions of others is to suppose that our wishes can count as reasons for others to act.

But we have yet to explain how it is that a request generates a reason for action. I want now to argue that one way in which requests generate reasons for action parallels the way promises generate reasons, which I described earlier. Just as a promisor has reason to keep a promise, since to renege would be to make a fool of the promisee, so, I want to argue, a requestee has reason to act in accordance with a request, because to fail to do so would be to make a fool of the requestor. It is not enough, of course, for the requestor merely to *become* a fool, that is, merely to come to have an unwarranted false belief. If the argument is to succeed, we must show that it is the requestee who is responsible for the requestor's false belief if the requestee does not treat the request as providing a reason for action.

Consider the position of a person contemplating making a request. Such a person faces a dilemma similar to that faced by a promisee: to avoid the risk of doing an injustice, the would-be requestor has to believe that, if the request were made, it would be viewed by the requestee as providing a reason for action. The possible injustice here is that of treating the would-be requestee as cold and indifferent, when he is not. To avoid the risk of injustice the would-be requestor must trust that the requestee will view the request as providing a reason for action. But, as for the promisee, this course of action carries the risk of becoming a fool. To illustrate, consider the relationship between a beggar and a passer-by. If the passer-by fails to regard the existence of the beggar's request as generating a reason to give, then the passer-by makes a fool of the beggar—makes false the beggar's (unwarranted) belief—if the beggar believed that the passer-by would regard the request as generating a reason to give. And the passer-by is responsible for the beggar's false belief, because the beggar must believe that the passer-by will regard the existence of the request as generating a reason for action if the beggar is to avoid the risk of doing the passer-by an injustice, the injustice of treating the passer-by as cold and indifferent when he is not.

Notice that although a requestor must trust, to avoid the risk of doing an injustice, this is not so in the case of a person who merely expresses a wish. To express a wish need not be an attempt to affect the action of another, and so does not imply that the person to whom the expression is made is not cold, not indifferent.

It is appropriate to speak of the requestor trusting here: a requestor's firm belief will not be fully warranted by the evidence. The belief that our requestee will treat our request as providing a reason for action is a belief about the response of a free agent. It is always an open question whether our request will be taken to provide a reason for action. But it is not simply that we are dealing here with the actions of free and rational agents. When we trust a person not to renege on a promise we are usually trusting the promisor not to accede to the temptation to act self-interestedly rather than keep the promise. Similarly, when we request and trust a person to regard our request as providing a reason for action, we are usually trusting that person not to accede to the temptation of self-interest. It is the fragility with which we resist, when indeed we do resist, acting in our own self-interest that makes a belief that self-interest will be resisted one of trust.

It is a presumption of the argument that a disposition to regard the wishes of others as a reason for action is a virtue, and that a person who has such a caring or loving disposition is superior to one who does not. I shall not argue for this claim. Of course, the argument would have little interest if this were a disposition which few regarded as a virtue. But that is not so. The presumption is that a disposition to regard the wishes of others as a reason to act is a virtue, but we need

not suppose that to be excessively concerned with the wishes
of others is a virtue. Indeed, a person who is too ready to act
in accordance with the wishes of others may be described as
servile, fawning, obsequious—and these dispositions are not
virtues. The virtue of treating the wishes of others as a reason
for action, of being caring and warm, may be viewed as a
mean between two failings: being uncaring, cold, indifferent,
and unloving on the one hand, and being too caring and hence
servile and subservient on the other.

But there is an obvious objection. A promise, we might say,
is initiated by a promisor: the promisor chooses to promise,
thereby setting the dilemma for the promisee. It may seem
reasonable, then, to say that the promisor owes it to the
promisee to solve the dilemma which he has created. But,
the objection goes, although a request is initiated by the
requestor, it is the requestee who, according to my argument,
comes to have the obligation. But if it is the requestor who
creates the dilemma by making the request, why should the
requestee be held responsible for solving the dilemma? Why
should the requestee be responsible for the requestor's becoming a fool, when the requestor could have avoided becoming
a fool by not making the request in the first place?

Now it is, of course, true that if the requestor had not made
the request, then the requestee would have faced no dilemma.
But it is a mistake to suppose that a requestor has a (morally)
free hand in deciding whether to make a request or not, for
there are moral risks in *not* making a request; hence it is a mistake to cast the requestor in the role of initiator, at least in any
morally significant sense. A person who contemplates making
a request but decides not to do so because she believes her
request will count for nothing does not avoid doing an injustice if the prospective requestee would have regarded the
request as providing a reason for action. Such an action, or
inaction, treats the would-be requestee as less than he is.

Thus would-be requestors may need to trust that their
requests will be thought to give rise to a reason for action,
and to act accordingly. But if this is so, then the would-be
requestor cannot escape the dilemma (of risking an injustice,

or becoming a fool) simply by not making a request. Certainly the requestee is not responsible for the requestor's having this dilemma—the requestor's dilemma is not brought about by the actions of the requestee. Nevertheless, the situation of the would-be requestor is one in which she can avoid the risk of doing an injustice only by making the request. And this situation, we may suppose, is one she has not brought upon herself. The issue here is not whether the case for holding the requestee responsible for the requestor's false belief is as compelling as the case for holding the promisor responsible for the false belief of the promisee; the issue is whether it is a satisfactory case for holding the requestee responsible. I suggest that it is.

But the idea that a person, simply by making a request, can immediately put us under an obligation is difficult to swallow. Suppose we are requested to do something which we should not do? Does a request to engage in, or assist with, torture, murder, or rape provide any reason to comply? Certainly in most, and perhaps in all, circumstances such requests should not be made. But it does not seem to follow from this that if the request has been made, there is no reason to comply with it. We should note, however, that a parallel problem arises with promises. Does a promise (given without ignorance or duress) to do something we ought not to do provide any reason to act in conformity with the promise? We may agree that we should not have made such a promise. But having made it, do we have any reason to keep it? If requests and promises are on all fours on this issue it is not specifically a problem for an argument that requests can generate obligations.

But in any case the argument I have given does not imply that all requests generate obligations. Earlier we identified two qualifications applying to the argument about promising, and these qualifications have their counterparts in the case of requests. Firstly, the argument I have given applies only where the requestor trusts the requestee to treat the request as providing a reason for action. In the absence of such trust there is no (unwarranted) belief for the requestee to make false. Of course it is not always easy to know whether a requestor does indeed trust; but there are forms of behaviour which count for, and others which count against, a presumption of trust. Reliance can often be evidence of trust, declining to rely of mistrust. To issue a wide appeal when compliance by only a few is required, or to prepare to use force to ensure that a person acts in accordance with a request, may betray a lack of trust.

Secondly, just as we may argue that, on some occasions, there is no obligation to keep a promise (grounded on the duty not to dupe), because to keep the promise would be to exhibit an excessive degree of trustworthiness, so, we may argue, on some occasions there is no obligation (grounded on a duty not to dupe) to act on a request, because to do so would be to exhibit an excessively caring disposition. Where a requestee would exhibit not merely a caring but a subservient disposition if he were to treat the request as providing a reason for action, the argument again unravels. A would-be requestor is not required, on pain of doing an injustice, to treat a potential requestee as not merely caring, but subservient. (Indeed to treat people as subservient if they are not is itself unjust.) Thus if a requestor makes a request which only a subservient requestee would regard as providing a reason for action, and believes that the request will be treated as providing a reason for action, then the requestor is responsible for holding a false belief if the request is not so treated. As with promising, the caveat rests on acceptance of the claim that the relevant virtue is a mean between two failings. If we deny this we must reject this qualification.

An understanding of the notion of subservience is, clearly, crucial to an understanding of when requests generate obligations in the manner I have described. I shall not attempt to give an account here. Certainly we may say that to expect others to give more concern to one's wishes than to their own is, on the face of it, to treat them as subservient. Thus, in general, a request for something to which one attaches no great importance generates no reason to act on the request if such action would be a significant inconvenience. And if I am not to treat you as subservient, then, if I believe that my request generates a reason for you to act, I must believe that a similar request from you in similar circumstances would generate a reason for me to act.

The argument I have given, if sound, shows that we can have reason to act in accordance with a request. This reason arises out of the very nature of a request, and parallels that which we may have for acting in accordance with a promise. If it is appropriate to speak of an obligation arising in the case of a promise in the manner I have described—and I suggest it is—why should it be inappropriate to speak of an obligation arising in the case of a request? Certainly, any requirement that there be a previous committing action is satisfied. Further, this reason for action generated by a request is grounded on the duty not to degrade and thus wrong the requestor. We may be reluctant to believe that requests can generate obligations, believing that we can never wrong anyone simply by failing to regard a request as generating a reason for action. But if my argument is valid, we must accept that such reluctance is misplaced.

4.3 *A Request Theory of Political Obligation*

The problem of finding a satisfactory basis for political obligation has a long history. But the problem becomes particularly acute in the modern period with the growth of what may loosely be termed individualism, and the conviction that we have no obligations except those we impose upon ourselves. Within this context an appeal to a social contract is natural enough. If successful, the contractarian approach would enable the obligation of the individual to obey to be derived without compromising the ultimate sovereignty of the individual, for the obligation to obey would indeed be one which individuals have imposed upon themselves.

The strengths of the contractarian approach are its respect for the sovereignty of the individual, and its derivation of political obligation from a promissory act. For, though explaining how it is that a promise obliges has seemed a problem to many, few have seriously doubted that promises do indeed create obligations—at least where there is no material ignorance, duress, or lack of competence. Yet the contractarian approach faces notorious difficulties. Although individuals might have an obligation if they have contracted, it seems doubtful that many ever do contract, either expressly or tacitly. And a mere hypothetical contract seems, for the purposes of generating an obligation at least, little better than no contract at all. Perhaps these (and other) difficulties can be overcome; I shall not pursue that question. Rather I want to suggest that, if requests do indeed create obligations, we may avoid the traditional problems associated with the contract theory by deriving political obligation not from a promise or contract, but from requests.

Once we admit that we may be placed under an obligation by the requests of others, it is plausible to suppose that, without regulation, we may be the recipients of innumerable conflicting requests. To avoid the dilemmas such a host of requests would create, we might argue, a co-ordinating agency is required; and in a democratic society the state might plausibly claim to be playing the role of such an agency. If this is so, then the obligation to comply with the laws of the state in a democratic society might be derived from viewing those laws as the collated and integrated requests which the different members of the society wish to make of one another.

Such an account would have a number of attractions. It would suggest how we might accommodate the conviction that democracy makes a difference to our political obligations, and without having to rely on the problematic claim that in a democracy most, if not all, citizens have consented to comply. Secondly, as we have seen, the theory will not support the claim that there is an obligation to act on a request where the requestee by acting would exhibit not merely a caring but a subservient disposition. This provision might be used to show that at least some unjust laws fail to generate any obligation to comply grounded on the duty not to dupe.

Such an account can be seen as going some way to meet the

claims of individualism. The account is consistent with some of the demands of individual sovereignty. The ultimate authority over each individual remains that individual: we are not to suppose that a requestor has a right to command. Nevertheless, a significant part of individualism is rejected, in particular the claim that we can have no obligations except those which we impose on ourselves. Request theory may, then, provide a means by which we may impose obligations upon each other, while at the same time recognizing each other as free and equal moral persons. (The theory offers a defence of political *obligation*, an obligation to do as we have been requested because we have been requested. It does not follow that a request theory can generate *authority*, a right to command. Indeed the appeal of a request theory is that it assumes no more than that we may be requested; and it is precisely because a request is not a command that this assumption is such a reasonable one to make.)

Nevertheless, such a theory is not without problems. In particular, we might wonder if the requirement that requestors trust their requestees if an obligation is to be generated is compatible with the use of coercive power by a state to ensure compliance with its laws. Or does the threat of force undermine the obligation to comply which laws, viewed as requests, might otherwise have generated? For a request theory to apply, those to whom the laws are addressed (usually citizens and aliens within a territory) must, it would seem, not be treated in ways which imply that they are not being trusted to act in accordance with the law. At first sight this may seem to imply that the state may not threaten. But perhaps this is too quick. To be sure, a police state is ruled out, but a state which operates through light policing may be able to claim that it is indeed trusting of its citizens, at least to some degree. Certainly there are significant limits on the kind of polity which is compatible with a political obligation based on a request theory. But the claim that just any state, irrespective of its character, is owed an obligation is a preposterous one.

5

Institutional Justice

IN this chapter I examine the nature of institutional justice, that is, the requirement to respect entitlements which arise from qualification under an established rule or institution. It is generally supposed that where some particular rule is in operation those who are denied that to which they are entitled under those rules are treated unjustly. The question I want to consider, then, is how this injustice is to be explained, and whether the explanation is consistent with understanding justice as a member of the fittingness family of concepts

Throughout the chapter I shall again set aside considerations of comparative injustice. Typically, ignoring entitlements involves comparative injustice for it is only some whose entitlements are ignored. If some, but only some, have their entitlements ignored, then it is plausible to say that all are not being treated as equals; and if all are indeed to be supposed equal, then the case will fall readily under justice as fittingness (1.5). But I shall assume that it is possible, at least in principle, for everyone's entitlements to be ignored, and that if they were this would be unjust. Of course we might doubt that in such a case it is still appropriate to speak of there being an established rule at all. But I shall assume that the case against justice as fittingness is as bad as it can be: that the injustice of ignoring entitlements is not (or not always) to be understood as only a comparative injustice.

I shall argue that the injustice of ignoring an entitlement is to be explained as a failure to treat in accordance with desert, and thus that there is no inconsistency with justice as fittingness. I shall also argue that often where there seems to be a clash between entitlement and desert we should respect entitlements—in order that all may have been treated in accordance with their deserts. But I begin with the problem of institutional justice itself, arguing that a number of putative solutions to the problem are unsatisfactory.

5.1 *The Problem of Institutional Justice*

Societies typically have established rules: practices, institutions, customs, and so on. Some of these rules we may wish to reject as unjust. Institutions may themselves be institutionally unjust (denying entitlements under higher ordered rules) or they may be non-institutionally unjust (unjust in a manner which does not rely on the notion of denying entitlements in accordance with rules at all). But where an institution is not itself unjust it is generally supposed to give rise to entitlements which it would be unjust to deny. Thus if, in a particular society, it is the practice to allocate places at universities on the basis of the results of a particular examination, then, assuming this practice is not unjust, to deny a place to the candidate who performs best in the examination would, other things being equal at least, be unjust.

Let us assume, then, that we are dealing with established rules which are not unjust. Why is it unjust to ignore entitlements under those rules? At first glance the answer may seem obvious. If the rules are just, then it may seem to be a requirement of justice that people receive in accordance with those rules. But this is to assume that the rules are not merely just but uniquely so, and this, as we noted earlier (2.3), is implausible. The more plausible view is that there is an indefinitely large set of (sets of) rules, all of which are not unjust. The question is, therefore, wherein lies the injustice in departing from some established, and not unjust, rule, and following, say, some other not unjust rule?

Our concern here is with justice. There are, usually, many good reasons to follow established rules. There are advantages attached to the adoption and implementation of a relatively stable system of rules, practices, and institutions. The stability and predictability of such a system add greatly to utility, and to the security and freedom of those to whom such rules and institutions are applied. These points are familiar enough and hardly require defence. But they do not show, immediately at least, that denying entitlements is unjust—as against inefficient, irrational, wasteful, or contrary to the promotion of human good.[1]

There is, to be sure, a certain congruency between justice which takes as given a set of rules, practices, and institutions, and justice viewed as a member of the fittingness family of

---

[1] Such considerations may also be appealed to in a less immediate argument. Rawls, for example, defends the rule of law on the ground that it is conducive to freedom: 'The principle of legality has a firm foundation, then, in the agreement of rational persons to establish for themselves the greatest equal liberty. To be confident in the possession and exercise of these freedoms, the citizens of a well-ordered society will normally want the rule of law maintained' (John Rawls, *A Theory of Justice* (Oxford, 1972), 239–40). If we can argue that justice requires maximizing equal freedom, then we can argue from justice, through freedom, to the respecting of entitlements. Such an argument will be consistent with justice as fittingness if maximizing equal freedom is required in order to treat all as equal and free (and if, as seems generally held, the freedom we are to be treated as possessing is status-conferring).

But there are a number of difficulties to be faced by such an argument. As Rawls acknowledges, we should expect that it is only *normally* that respecting entitlements will maximize equal freedom. The argument cannot, then, explain the injustice of denying entitlements when this will not preclude maximizing equal freedom. Indeed, even if maximizing equal freedom *always* required respecting existing (not unjust) entitlements, the argument would still be unable to explain why it would be unjust to ignore such entitlements even if this were not so. (The argument here parallels the rejection of utilitarianism as a basis on which to defend the injustice of slavery: even if we grant that slavery can never lead to a maximizing of utility, the utilitarian anti-slavery argument cannot explain why slavery would be unjust even if it did maximize utility.) Further, in so far as we rely on a consequentialist argument of this type it seems that we shall be unable to explain why the denial of entitlements is obviously unjust, as we usually suppose it to be. The argument is simply too indirect to do that.

Finally, the argument relies on the claim that maximizing equal freedom is indeed a requirement of justice—and even Rawls seems less than unequivocal on this point: 'if . . . lesser liberty is unnecessary and not imposed by some human agency, the scheme of liberty is to this degree *irrational rather than unjust*. Unequal liberty . . . is another matter and immediately raises a question of justice' (ibid. 229, emphasis added) For these reasons, then, it seems unwise to rely on an argument from freedom for the justice of respecting entitlements.

concepts: both require the avoidance of misclassification. And the tendency to speak not of injustice but of contempt and disrespect where authority to judge is denied (1.4) is mirrored, in the case of institutional justice, by a preference for speaking of the illegal rather than the unjust where requisite authority is absent. But the existence of such congruency neither provides a satisfactory explanation of why institutional injustice is indeed unjust, nor removes the problem which institutional entitlements pose for justice as fittingness, for when people are denied such entitlements the injustice is not merely an injustice *relative to some rule*. The injustice, it is generally supposed, goes deeper than that. To be sure, an institutional injustice depends for its existence on the existence of the institution: if there were no institution there would be no institutional injustice. But we cannot reject the claim that a given institutional injustice is a genuine injustice simply on the basis of *any* rejection of the institution. (Assuming an institution is not unjust, we should accept that people are treated unjustly if they are denied what they are entitled to under that institution, even if the institution is one which, say on grounds of efficiency, we believe should be abandoned.) And this deeper injustice mere congruency cannot explain. What we require, then, is an explication of institutional injustice in terms of non-institutional injustice.

I want now to consider whether we may explain the injustice of ignoring a rule-based entitlement by assimilating such entitlements to rights arising from promissory acts. An account of this type will, of course, need to rely on the claim that to be denied what one has been promised is to be treated unjustly and (if trivial circularity is to be avoided) for some reason other than that there is an established rule that promises be kept, and that justice requires treatment in accordance with established rules. I have not claimed that this is so, and, indeed, I have suggested (4.1) that the belief that (even in the absence of any promise-keeping institution) reneging on one's promises is wrong is consistent with a denial that reneging is always unjust. Nevertheless, let us suppose, for the sake of the argument, that reneging is indeed unjust (and not, or not only, an institutional injustice) and consider whether the injustice of ignoring institutional entitlements can be accounted for as a violation of a promissory act.

The issue, then, is whether a person who qualifies under an established rule has been promised. Now it may be that on *some* occasions a person who has qualified under a rule has been promised, but the question is whether to qualify under an established rule is, *ipso facto*, at least normally, to have been promised. This seems extremely doubtful. There are a number of difficulties such an argument would face.

Firstly, there is the problem of showing that, where a practice is being followed, a promise has been made, rather than, at most, an intention has been indicated. It is uncontroversial to say that promises create obligations; but it is far from clear that the mere expression of an intention to act creates an obligation.

Secondly, it is generally supposed that to make a binding promise it is necessary to understand the significance of what one is doing, or to have been culpably negligent in failing to discover that significance. But it seems that no such understanding is required for established rules to give rise to entitlements. A society may follow rules without any member being aware of the rules which are being followed: there may be rules which have never been consciously adopted nor ever called into question. Yet there seems no reason to suppose that such rules, providing they are not unjust, do not generate entitlements just as consciously adopted rules do.

Thirdly, the promissory account faces a difficulty arising from the fact that a promise provides a reason for action only for the promisor. If we suppose that an established rule represents the promise only of those who have authority to change the rules in a given society, then the promissory account can explain only the injustice of ignoring entitlements by those in authority. And even if we suppose the established rules to represent the promise of an entire society, we will still be unable to explain why it would be unjust for non-members of that society to ignore entitlements which arise from established rules. But, providing once again that the rules themselves are not unjust, it seems unjust for non-members to ignore entitlements arising from established rules. The promissory account, then, seems unable to explain the universality of the requirement to respect rule-based entitlements. At the very least such an account seems incomplete.

Thus the attempt to account for the injustice of ignoring entitlements by assimilation to rights arising from promises seems strained at a number of points. The claim that those who are entitled have always been promised seems a fiction, and the entitlement deriving from an established rule seems, at least sometimes, to have a different form, and different consequences, from that which we associate with entitlements deriving from promissory acts.

An argument which maintains the spirit of the promissory account, but avoids problems of the former type, is this: although those who are entitled under established rules may not have been promised, they have entitlements *as if* they had been promised. Just as a promisee is led to expect that which has been promised, so, it might be argued, where there are established rules, people are led to expect that for which they qualify under the rules.

But this too seems a doubtful argument. In the first place, the argument seems unable to explain why it is unjust to deny the entitlements of those who do not expect to have their entitlements honoured. But we usually suppose that the denial of such entitlements is unjust. Secondly, we may reasonably doubt whether the major premiss of the argument is true, that is, we may reasonably doubt that there is any duty to fulfil expectations one has generated. If I (honestly) tell you that I confidently expect to do X but do not promise, then although I lead you to expect me to do X, I may reasonably deny that I incur any obligation to do X. Perhaps it will be said that there is something in this argument: perhaps in so far as I lead someone to expect a particular action I am under some (albeit weak) obligation to perform that action. But even this argument seems unable to account for the injustice of ignoring entitlements: a weak obligation seems hardly sufficient to ground the relatively strong claims which derive from established rules.[2]

I conclude that the attempt to ground rule-based entitlements by assimilating them to rights based on promissory or quasi-promissory acts faces grave difficulties. It may be that many of those who have such entitlements can also claim entitlement on the basis of promissory obligation. But it seems plausible to suppose that the injustice of ignoring an entitlement based on qualification under an established rule *per se* has a different source.

---

[2] An alternative argument which appeals to expectations (which have not been generated by promissory acts) is offered by Rawls: 'In a well-ordered society individuals acquire claims to a share of the social product by doing certain things which are encouraged by the existing arrangements. The legitimate expectations that arise are the other side, so to speak, of the principle of fairness and the natural duty of justice. For in the way that one has a duty to uphold just arrangements, and an obligation to do one's part when one has accepted a position in them, so a person who has complied with the scheme and done his share has a right to be treated accordingly by others. They are bound to meet his legitimate expectations. Thus when just economic arrangements exist, the claims of individuals are properly settled by reference to the rules and precepts (with their respective weights) which these practices take as relevant' (ibid. 313).

If respect for rule-based entitlements is to be grounded on the principle of fairness (and if the principle of fairness is grounded on the duty to treat equals as equals), then the requirement to respect entitlements is rendered consistent with justice as fittingness. But again it seems unwise to rely on this argument. In the first place, although the principle of fairness may provide a ground for respecting institution-based entitlements where the principle applies, there seems good reason to suppose that it is unjust to ignore entitlements which arise from (not unjust) institutions where the principle of fairness does not apply; and this injustice cannot, of course, be accounted for by the principle of fairness. And further, it seems doubtful whether the principle of fairness applies very widely. Certainly individuals do not generally participate in social and economic arrangements in the voluntary manner required for the mere acceptance of benefits to count as generating obligations, including the obligation to recognize the alleged legitimate expectations of others. (If I am to be required to bear certain burdens whether I accept benefits or not, my acceptance of benefits can hardly be used as a ground to justify that requirement.)

As regards the argument from the natural duty of justice, we are assuming that the existing rules are just, but not uniquely so. Why, then, should it be thought that the natural duty of justice requires that we act in accordance with *existing* just rules? Simply to assume that there is a natural duty of justice to act in accordance with existing arrangements where they are just would be to beg the question at issue.

5.2 *The Reduction of Entitlement to Desert*

I want now to consider whether the injustice of ignoring entitlements can be explained in terms of desert. If we fail to honour people's entitlements, do we thereby fail to treat them in
accordance with their deserts? The simplest way of defending
this view would be to argue that qualification under a rule can
function as a desert basis. But this seems a non-starter—at
least if we accept the status requirement. It may be that 'having qualified for' may count as a fact about the subject, but it
is highly implausible to suppose that merely qualifying under
a rule affects the status of the qualifier. We do not become
more worthy of respect, we are not elevated, simply by virtue
of the fact that we satisfy the requirements of some rule. This
is not to deny that some rules are satisfied by the possession
of an attribute which is status-affecting. But where this is so it
is the possession of the attribute which enables a person to
qualify under a rule, not the *qualifying under a rule*, which
affects status. (The relationship between qualification under a
rule and the possession of any status-affecting attributes is
wholly contingent upon the content of the rule.) Thus being
entitled cannot function as a desert basis, and we do not
deserve simply because we are entitled.

However, even if a direct argument would fail, it may still
be possible to reduce entitlements to deserts, albeit in a less
direct manner. What is required is an argument which is based
on no more than the bare recognition of a rule: we cannot
argue from the content or source of rules, for entitlements
derive from rules with various sources and having diverse
content. I will now sketch such argument.

The nub of the argument is that the existence of rules (customs, practices, institutions)—including the rules from which
entitlements derive—may affect the meaning of an action. In
particular, the existence of a rule may affect whether a particular action constitutes a (particular) piece of treatment, and
an action which, in the absence of a rule or custom, may sig-
nify nothing may come to have a meaning by virtue of the

existence of an established rule or custom. Where there is a rule that shoes must be removed before entering a temple, to enter wearing shoes is a way of treating irreverently. A man may treat a church with disrespect by wearing a hat because, and only because, of the existence of a custom that men are to remove their hats on entering churches. Women cannot treat churches with contempt in this way simply because there is no comparable established custom in their case.

Now this is relevant to desert for, as we have seen (2.1), the relationship between what is deserved and the desert basis involves treatment: to say that S deserves X is to say the allotting of X to S is a means of treating S as having the desert basis in question. When we deserve, what we deserve, we deserve as a (particular) treatment. If punishments are deserved they are deserved, as a means of treating those punished as wrongdoers. If a candidate for a university place is the most able, has worked the hardest, and so on, and that candidate is said therefore to deserve the place, then awarding the place to that candidate is a way of treating that candidate as the most able, as having worked hardest, and so on.

To illustrate how the existence of a rule may affect what constitutes a particular piece of treatment, and thereby what is required in order to treat in accordance with deserts, consider the case of two applicants, Alan and Brian, who are in competition for a single place at a university. Suppose that Alan is the more able, has worked harder, has had fewer advantages, and so on. Whatever we take to be the relevant attributes for deserving the place, Alan has them and Brian does not. Thus we may say that Alan deserves the place, Brian does not.

But now suppose the university establishes a practice of holding an entrance examination and allocating places on the basis of the marks achieved. Suppose we accept that such a practice is not unjust. The two applicants take the examination and Brian achieves the higher marks: he is fortunate that precisely those questions he has anticipated are on the paper. Now doing well (by good fortune) in the examination has not made Brian any more worthy of respect or admiration. It is not a basis for amending our appraisal of him; it has not affected his status. In short, scoring the higher marks (in this way) has not made Brian any more deserving.

Nevertheless, Brian is now entitled to the place, and to deny it to him, we may say, would be unjust. Why would it be unjust? The point is that the existence of the custom or rule that the person scoring the higher marks be allocated the place changes what is expressed by the allocating of the place. Suppose that the place is allocated to Alan, but that there is no reason to suppose that the rule itself has been disestablished. How are we to understand the meaning of such an act? How should we view Brian as having been treated?

I want to suggest that such an action no longer treats Brian merely as someone who, on the basis of his abilities and so on, does not deserve the place; to depart from the established rule is to treat Brian as if he were someone who deserves not to have the place. Now it is true that Brian does not deserve the place, but it may be false that he deserves not to have it. If Brian really does deserve not to have the place it will not be unjust to deny it to him. If, for example, he has attempted to burn down the library, we might think he deserves not to have the place. (Allowing him to take the examination is, of course, a reason to believe that he is not thought to deserve not to have the place.) But if it is not the case that Brian deserves not to have the place—if he merely does not deserve it—then to deny the place to him is unjust. And it is unjust because it is to treat him as deserving not to have the place when, in fact, it is not true that he deserves not to have it. It is to treat him as having deserts he does not have, and hence not in accordance with his deserts.

This is to put the argument in its Sverdlikian form, relying on the claim that we can act unjustly towards people who have no deserts—by treating them as if they have deserts they do not have. If we take the Kleinigian view and say that where people are undeserving—have no relevant deserts—then nothing follows as to what they should or should not get, we must include an additional stage. If Brian is denied his entitlement, then he is treated as deserving not to be allocated the place. That is, he is treated as possessing some status-affecting attribute (call it Q), which is the desert basis for his deserving not to receive the place. But, *ex hypothesi*, Brian does not possess Q. That is, he is innocent of Q. But if Q is status-affecting, so too is innocence of Q. On the basis of his innocence of Q, therefore, Brian deserves, in the context of the rules, to be allocated the place. A failure to allocate the place to Brian is unjust, and it is unjust because it fails to treat him in accordance with his desert. (The desert basis is not, of course, effort or ability; it is his being innocent of any (adequate) basis for his deserving not to be allocated the place.)

The central point of the argument is a simple one: when we are deliberately denied what we have qualified for under established rules—in circumstances where the relevant rule has not been disestablished—we are treated as someone to whom that which has been qualified for should be denied. The argument relies, of course, on our being able to draw a distinction between failing to follow, and disestablishing or abandoning, a rule. This distinction seems clear enough in theory, even if it may sometimes be difficult in practice to determine which description is appropriate.

Now it may be objected that to allocate the place to Alan is not to treat Brian as deserving not to be allocated the place; rather it is simply to treat Alan as deserving the place. We might say that we must weigh Alan's desert claim against Brian's entitlement, and that to allocate the place to Alan is simply to treat Alan's claim as the stronger. This may be unusual, and even indefensible, the objection runs, but it is not to treat Brian as deserving not to be allocated the place.

But such an objection overlooks the fact that the existence of an established rule affects not only what Brian must receive if he is to be treated in accordance with his deserts: it also changes what Alan must receive if he is to have been treated in accordance with his deserts. Alan is the more able, the more hard-working, and so on. He deserves to be treated as such. In the absence of the practice of allocating places on the basis of an entrance examination, allocating the place to Alan would, we have supposed, treat him as he deserves to be treated. Indeed it may be the only way so to treat him, and if that is so, it follows that, in the absence of the practice, it would be unjust, other things being equal at least, to deny it to him.

But to the extent that the rule of allocating on the basis of an entrance examination is established, the allocation of a place is no longer a way of treating someone (the recipient) as able, hard-working, and so on. It is, rather, a way of treating someone as the most successful in the entrance examination. Thus, although Alan is the more able, and although he may have deserts on this basis, it cannot be said that he must receive the place if he is to have been treated according to his deserts. What justice requires is that Alan is not treated as not the most able, hard-working, and so on. A refusal to commiserate with Alan on his ill fortune (where such commiseration would, if appropriate, be expected—say by a friend) would be such a way of treating him, and would be unjust. But given an established practice of allocating on the basis of an entrance examination, allocating the place to Alan can no longer be viewed as required in order to treat him as the most able, and so on. Thus we may not interpret the allocating of the place to Alan as simply treating Alan as deserving the place—rather than as treating Brian as deserving not to be allocated the place—for given the established rule, Alan no longer deserves the place.

Thus the standard view of conflicts between entitlements and deserts seems misconceived. The usual view is that claims of desert and claims of entitlement are distinct, and may conflict. Faced with such conflict, at least in general, entitlements must triumph over deserts. And thus, at least in societies where there are—or are thought to be—entitlements to most things, desert has little role except, perhaps, in determining (or in helping to determine) which rules, customs, and institutions ought to exist.

But if we accept the reductive argument I have outlined, this view is mistaken in all essentials. If the claims of entitlement are ultimately grounded on treating in accordance with desert, then, paradoxical as it may at first sight appear, in cases where, supposedly, entitlement triumphs over desert, the ultimate justification of our action is the requirement that all are treated in accordance with their deserts. And given that the establishment of a rule changes what is required if people are to be treated in accordance with their (pre-institutional) deserts—as when Alan's desert ceased to require the allocation of the place for its satisfaction—it is a misdescription to say, in cases where it seems that entitlement triumphs over desert, that desert has been trumped and counts for little. Claims of entitlement are grounded, ultimately, on desert, and the pre-institutional desert claims with which they might be supposed to clash do not—given the established rule—conflict at all. Contrary to appearances, then, there is no clash in such cases, and what treating in accordance with desert requires, given the existence of the rule, is allocation in accordance with entitlement. The injustice of ignoring entitlement, and the priority of entitlements over pre-institutional desert, can all be explained by appealing to the principle that all are to be treated in accordance with their deserts.

Indeed to speak of weighing desert and entitlement in this context, as if these were competing independent claims, is misleading. To the extent that there are genuine entitlement claims to X, there are not genuine pre-institutional desert claims to X, and vice versa. The claim that it would be unjust to ignore an entitlement to X rests on the claim that there is indeed an established rule from which it follows (and that this rule is not unjust). To the extent that we think that there is a genuine pre-institutional desert claim to X we must think that the rule is not fully established (or that it is unjust). We may wish to equivocate: we may wish to say that the rule is only to some degree established. But if we do, we should at least admit that this is the source of any dilemma. It is not that there are independent rival claims, each of which is beyond reproach.

This reductive argument, then, if successful, shows why we cannot ignore entitlements if we are to avoid injustice. It shows also that, although the notions of entitlement and desert are distinct, it does not follow that the injustice of ignoring entitlements is not based on a requirement that people be treated in accordance with their deserts. Thus we may accept the importance, for justice, of rule-based entitlements without abandoning the view that justice requires only treatment in accordance with desert. I conclude that recognizing entitlements is no bar to accepting justice as fittingness.

6

Punishment and Reward

IN this chapter I discuss the practices of rewarding and punishing, and examine their relationship to justice. I do not attempt either to offer a defence of these practices, or to argue that no defence can be given: my objectives are more limited. My main aim is to consider whether justice as fittingness provides a satisfactory framework within which to discuss the relationship between justice and the practices of rewarding and punishing. How far are arguments about the justice of rewarding or punishing (and of failing to reward or punish) compatible with the claim that injustice is to be understood in terms of unfitting treatment? I also consider what, if anything, accepting justice as fittingness commits us to as far as punishment and reward are concerned. I have claimed that desert is central to justice (2.1), and, as I shall discuss later (7.4), there is a close association between desert and the notions of reward and punishment. It may seem, therefore, that to accept justice as fittingness is to accept that reward and punishment have a particularly significant role to play in a just society, and even that to accept justice as fittingness is to be committed to retributivism. In this chapter I consider whether this so.

I proceed in the following way. I begin by discussing the notions of reward and punishment, explaining how I shall understand these terms. I then consider when, if ever, it is unjust not to punish or reward. When, if ever, are punishments or rewards required as a matter of justice? The issue here is whether rewarding and punishing are discretionary practices (2.2) or practices which a society must adopt if it is to be just. Finally, I consider when punishing and rewarding are compatible with justice. When may we punish or reward without acting unjustly?

Throughout I set aside entitlements and considerations of comparative justice. If people are entitled to rewards, or entitled not to be punished, then we may argue that they are unjustly treated if their entitlements are ignored. Similarly, to punish or reward some while refusing to punish or reward others, where the circumstances are no different, will be unjust if it is to treat some as less than they are relative to others. I have discussed entitlement and comparative justice and I will not add to that discussion here. Certainly in deciding how we should act we need to take entitlements and comparative considerations into account, but such considerations are not concerned specifically with rewarding and punishing. My concern, then, will be with the question of when it is non-comparatively unjust to reward and punish, and to fail to reward and punish, leaving aside any entitlement-generating rules.

6.1 *The Practices of Punishing and Rewarding*

Before discussing the relationship between punishing and rewarding, and justice, we need to have on hand an account of what rewards and punishments are. I shall assume that when speaking of rewarding and punishing we are referring to practices which combine the following elements: an act of rewarding or punishing is, or purports to be, a reaction to (respectively) right- or wrongdoing (including by omission) which treats the person rewarded or punished as (respectively) a right- or wrongdoer, and does so by imposing or allotting what is intended to be (respectively) welcome or unwelcome to the recipient.

It is plausible to view rewards and punishments as reactions, and, in particular, as reactions to actions (or omissions). To view rewards and punishments in this way is, we might say, to take a retributive view of what these practices are. (This is a view about what these practices are—a view we may take even if we reject a retributive account of the justification for engaging in these practices.) An action done in response to, say, an event or state of affairs would lack the symmetry of a reaction to an action. Such a lack of symmetry would tend to undermine any alleged appropriateness of the response, but would also tend to undermine our understanding of the rewarding or punishing as a *reaction*. Rewards and punishments become not only less defensible but less intelligible when they are imposed for what people are, not for what people do. (People who are evil or malicious should be treated as such, but they should only be punished for what they do, not simply for being evil.)

Rewarding and punishing are, then, to be understood as reactions: as actions done in response to other actions. But more than this they are, at least in central cases, ways of reacting which give expression to a belief that the action to which they are a response was a right or wrong action.[1] To punish is to imply that the punished action was wrong: to treat the person punished as a wrongdoer. (The use of 'correction' for punishment makes this connection explicit.) To reward is to treat the person rewarded as a rightdoer; to imply that the action to which it is a response was a right action.

We may react to a right or wrong action, treating the agent as a right- or wrongdoer, without rewarding or punishing. We may commend, applaud, acclaim, or praise; and we may denounce, reproach, condemn, admonish, reprimand, or rebuke. Rewarding and punishing differ from these forms of treatment by virtue of the fact that to reward is intentionally to bestow something which is thought to be, and normally is, advantageous, beneficial, and welcome, while to punish is intentionally to make suffer, intentionally to inflict something disadvantageous, burdensome, and unwelcome. We may anticipate that our commendation will in itself be welcome, and our condemnation in itself unwelcome. But we may commend without intending to benefit, condemn without intending to

---

[1] Cf. Joel Feinberg, 'The Expressive Function of Punishment', in *Doing and Deserving* (Princeton, 1970), 95–118, and A. J. Skillen, 'How to Say Things with Walls', *Philosophy*, 55 (1980), 509–23.

make suffer. To commend is not in itself to reward, and to condemn is not in itself to punish.

Offering what would be welcome, or threatening what would be unwelcome, are ways of attempting to affect behaviour. The offer of a reward and the threat of punishment may normally be expected to affect behaviour. But rewarding and punishing differ from other behaviour-affecting practices by virtue of the first element we have noted: to reward is to treat as a rightdoer, to punish, as a wrongdoer. Where we attempt to affect action but without implying that the action will be right or wrong we give not rewards but mere incentives, inducements, or bribes; not punishments but penalties, disincentives, and deterrents. (Punishments are to be contrasted with penalties: to call a burden a penalty is not to imply that the action penalized is wrong. Thus we may speak of penalties for the early repayment of a loan or the cashing of a life insurance policy.[2]) It is not part of the essential nature of rewards and punishments that they affect behaviour; rather it is a normal and generally anticipated effect. It is possible to reward and punish even where there is no prospect of affecting the future actions of those so treated, or of others. The fact that rewarding and punishing can, normally, be expected to affect behaviour is simply a consequence of the fact that people (and animals), other things being equal, tend to seek to obtain what is advantageous and welcome, and avoid what is disadvantageous and burdensome.

It has been suggested that punishment is essentially a defeat for those who are punished.[3] But this view too should be rejected. The imposition of punishment is the imposition of something which, in itself, is intended to be unwelcome. As just noted, we normally seek to avoid what is unwelcome, and the imposition of punishment may, therefore, normally

---

[2] Here I follow Feinberg, 'The Expressive Function of Punishment', 97–8.

[3] '. . . the most general and accurate definition of punishment is the experience of defeat at the hands (either directly or indirectly through legal authority) of the victim' (Jean Hampton, 'A New Theory of Retribution' in R. G. Frey and Christopher Morris (eds.), *Liability and Responsibility: Essays in Law and Morals* (Cambridge, 1991), 399).

6. Punishment and Reward   141

constitute a defeat. But this is not always so. The remorseful wrongdoer who wishes to be punished, perhaps hoping that such punishment will go some way towards expiating guilt, is not defeated when punished. The punishment is welcomed, though the punishment involves the imposition of what in itself is unwelcome. Thus punishment can be a defeat, but need not be, just as a reward need not be a victory.

I claimed earlier (1.4) that to call an act just or unjust is to suggest that the person acting does not lack any necessary authority to judge. This tendency has its parallel in the case of rewarding and punishing: to call something a reward or punishment is to suggest that those who bestow or allot are not disqualified from passing judgement. It is not that we cannot speak of children punishing or rewarding their parents, or of our punishing or rewarding God. We can, and such descriptions are not unintelligible. It is simply that in so doing we tend to imply that there is no incompetence to judge, no lack of requisite authority.[4]

This account of the notions of reward and punishment makes clear that reward and punishment are a 'neat contrasting' pair.[5] This being so it is appropriate to discuss rewarding with punishing. To be avoided is the view that rewards are a part of social justice (primarily concerned with the distribution of benefits) which is radically distinct from the justice of punishment. Such an organization fails to reflect the more significant divisions and associations. The distinction between the just distribution of benefits on the one hand, and the just distribution of burdens on the other, is superficial when compared with distinctions based on differing reasons for their allocation. Of course in determining how what is welcome and beneficial is to be distributed we will need to take into account any rewards which are required, and these rewards will need to be imposed upon whatever are the requirements of justice leaving rewards aside. At least some of these requirements I discussed earlier (3.1–3). But this is true for

---

[4] Cf. Anthony Flew, 'The Justification of Punishment', in H. B. Acton (ed.), *The Philosophy of Punishment* (London, 1969), 86–7.
[5] Joel Feinberg, *Doing and Deserving*, 67.

punishments too: if justice requires that such burdens as fines, community service, and hard labour be imposed as punishments, a just distribution of burdens which has left punishment aside will need to be amended to include such punishments.

6.2 *The Justice of Failing to Punish and Reward*

Does justice require that the practices of punishing and rewarding be adopted? Is a failure to punish or reward ever unjust? Failing to punish or reward will be unjust if wrongdoers deserve to be punished, or rightdoers deserve to be rewarded, and justice requires that all are treated according to their deserts. That such failures are, or can be, unjust—as regards punishment, at least—is the view taken by retributivists: those who do wrong deserve punishment as retribution for their wrongdoing.

The problem faced by retributivists is clear enough. To treat those who are not wrongdoers as if they are, or those who are rightdoers as if they are not, is to do an injustice. And to treat wrongdoers as if they are not wrongdoers, or those who are not rightdoers as if they are, is contrary to justice. But, as we have noted (6.1), punishing is not the only means by which a wrongdoer may be treated as a wrongdoer, nor rewarding the only way to treat a rightdoer as a rightdoer. Why, then, should we say that it is punishments and rewards which are deserved? How can a failure to punish or reward necessarily be unjust? Wherein lies the injustice if the wrongdoer is merely censured, the rightdoer merely acclaimed?

To punish is to make suffer, to reward is to bestow a benefit. The imposition of suffering clearly calls for justification. But so too does the use of resources to reward. Where there is any degree of scarcity the use of resources to reward may preclude their use for other purposes (for incentives, say). And even where there is no scarcity, the use of benefits to reward necessitates, in principle at least, the denial of those benefits (or those benefits to the same degree) to those who are not to be rewarded. Thus the use of benefits and burdens in the treating of rightdoers as rightdoers, wrongdoers as wrongdoers, calls for justification: it is not enough to justify only the commendation and censuring aspects of rewarding and punishing.[6] To show that rewarding and punishing are required by justice it is necessary to show that rewarding and punishing, in all their aspects, are required by justice.[7] The task, then, is to show that punishing and rewarding, involving as they do the intentional infliction of suffering and the intentional bestowal of benefits, are peculiarly appropriate responses to wrong- and rightdoing.

It is insufficient to assert that it is fitting or appropriate that the wicked should suffer, the virtuous prosper. There is no denying that for many there is an intuitive appropriateness when events follow this pattern. But an intuition of this kind is not a suitable basis from which to argue. Argument is required, and there are a number of forms which the necessary argument might take. I want to sketch some of these arguments, and to consider whether they are compatible with—indeed how far they rely on—the claim that justice is a fittingness concept.

It is useful to distinguish between arguments which rely on principles of justice which are rectificatory, and those which do not. Principles of rectificatory justice specify appropriate responses to already existing injustices. We speak in this context of putting right or undoing, annulling or cancelling out,

---

[6] Cf. C. L. Ten, *Crime, Guilt, and Punishment* (Oxford, 1987), 65.

[7] One of these aspects concerns the demonstration that some *particular* level of reward or punishment is required by justice: the problem of sentencing. As Burgh notes: 'in order to render punishment compatible with justice it is not enough to restrict punishment to the deserving, but we must, in addition, restrict the degree of punishment to the degree that is deserved' (Richard W. Burgh, 'Do the Guilty Deserve Punishment?', *Journal of Philosophy*, 79 (1982), 197). In addition, if justice requires the imposition of punishment, it also, presumably, requires the imposition of some minimum degree of punishment. Too little punishment is unjust, although there may be no one to whom it is unjust. The same points apply to rewards: too little treats the rewarded person unjustly, too much is unjust in the way that rewarding those who are unworthy is unjust. I shall not discuss these problems, but they must be faced by anyone who wishes to claim that justice requires that the practices of punishing and rewarding be adopted.

prior unjust actions, or the effects of such actions. We employ such notions as rebalancing, of correcting things which are out of joint, of setting things straight. Strategies for rectifying include paying reparations and making restitution, compensating (when done in response to prior injustice), and perhaps punishing. Non-rectificatory principles, by contrast, are concerned with the avoidance of injustice in the first place. These principles indicate what must be avoided if justice is not to be lost, whereas rectificatory principles indicate what must be done if justice is to be regained. Consider first some of the arguments for punishing and rewarding based on rectification and annulment.

Certainly it is often suggested that punishment can annul a crime, can set the record straight, and that those who are punished thereby pay their debt to society. Such claims employ the idea that punishment is justified because it rectifies by annulling. But can punishment really annul? We may agree that to speak in this way may serve a useful function in helping to rehabilitate offenders, and in healing the divisions caused by prior injustice. But can punishment really undo or annul past injustice? After all, there is an important sense in which what has been done cannot be undone at all, and even where it is possible to undo the effects of wrong actions this is to be achieved not by punishment, but by restitution, reparation, and compensation.

But there are some annulment arguments which deserve to be taken seriously, at least as regards the possible annulment of some wrongdoing. These include Morris's argument that punishment may restore a fair balance of benefits and burdens which the wrongdoer upsets;[8] and Hampton's argument that

---

[8] See Herbert Morris, 'Persons and Punishment', *Monist*, 52 (1968), 475–501. Morris does not claim that punishment is uniquely qualified to undo: 'Forgiveness—with its legal analogue of a pardon—while not the righting of an unfair distribution by making one pay his debt is, nevertheless, a restoring of the equilibrium by forgiving the debt' (p. 478). For discussion of this line of argument, see Burgh, 'Do the Guilty Deserve Punishment?', 193–210; George Sher, *Desert* (Princeton, 1987), ch. 5; Hampton, 'A New Theory of Retribution', esp. 384–6; and David Delinko, 'Some Thoughts on Retributivism', *Ethics*, 101 (1991), esp. 545–9.

punishment may be necessary to annul the false message of superiority implicit in a wrongdoer's treatment of a victim.[9] How far are such arguments compatible with justice as fittingness—indeed how far do they presuppose such a view of justice?

The nature of the original injustice which is to be annulled by the punishment will vary with differing annulment arguments. There is no reason in principle to suppose that this injustice is incompatible with understanding justice as a member of the fittingness family of concepts, and certainly the original injustices in the arguments of Morris and Hampton are readily understood as cases of unfitting treatment.[10] But

---

[9] See Hampton, 'A New Theory of Retribution', 377–414. For a discussion of the argument, see Delinko, 'Some Thoughts on Retributivism', esp. 549–54. Impressive as Hampton's argument is, it is not clear that it can deal with all the problems it faces. Possible difficulties include the following. Firstly, is it clear that annulment of the message is required? Does the argument here rest on a claim that to fail to punish is to accept the message, or condone the wrongdoing? If so, is this a defensible claim? After all, liberals have long argued that one may tolerate a practice without thereby implying approval of it. Secondly, does most punishment really annul the wrongdoing in the manner suggested? In particular, if it is not the victim who punishes the offender why does this not simply issue a new message of superiority—of, say, state over offender—rather than annul the supposed message of the offence? Thirdly, even if punishment will annul to some degree, and is permissible, is it the only method of annulling—or, at least, is punishment the only practical, permissible method of annulment? Can it be shown that advantaging the victim, or non-offender, is not a practical or permissible option? Fourthly, even if punishing does annul, at least to some degree, is it permissible? If we punish only to cancel a previous injustice to the victim, are we acting towards the offender in a manner which constitutes treating the offender simply as a means to an end—albeit the end of rectifying an injustice? (I discuss later (6.3) this type of objection to punishment.)

[10] As regards the argument from the annulment of an unfair distribution of benefits and burdens, in order to say that an action is unjust because it unbalances a prior fair distribution, we must have an understanding of what constitutes a fair distribution. We might claim that an equal (or unequal) distribution is fair on the grounds that people are equals (or unequals), and deserve to be treated as such. Alternatively we might claim that a particular distribution is fair because it treats in accordance with entitlement, contribution, need, and so on; but if the arguments presented earlier are sound, such considerations are reducible to desert. Thus we may argue that any prior fair distribution is to be understood as treatment in accordance with desert (and hence status), and thus that the action to be punished constitutes unfitting treatment. As regards Hampton's argument, the function

we may also argue that the claim that injustice requires rectification—the claim which all rectification arguments presuppose—is also to be explained by understanding justice as a
fittingness concept.

Suppose it is possible to argue that punishment, and only
punishment, does indeed annul past injustice. There is still the
question why we should suppose that justice requires the
annulment of past injustice—where, and to the extent that,
this is possible. One way to defend this claim is to argue that
where we leave injustice unrectified we leave the world
stained, out of joint, lacking the harmony which the unjust act
disrupts; and that this is simply something which we should
not do. But this approach seems less than satisfactory. It
seems, on the face of it, to rely heavily on aesthetic metaphors.
Perhaps this is something we should be willing to accept.[11]
But there are other problems: such an approach seems unable
to account for the belief that, at least sometimes, rectification
is owed specifically to those who have been done the injustice;
and it seems unable to account for the belief that those unjust
actions which treat people as *less* than they are are more serious than those which do not. At the very least, then, this argument for rectification seems to present less than the full case.

These problems can be overcome by arguing that the duty
to rectify past injustice, where, and to the extent, possible, is
based on a (more fundamental) non-rectificatory duty to
avoid doing injustice, because a refusal to rectify a past injustice constitutes a new injustice which compounds the original.
The new injustice is done where such a refusal (by someone
not lacking any requisite authority) treats the person done the
original injustice as a being to whom justice is not owed—
perhaps as a being lacking the capacity (or potentiality) for
consciousness of self and status, and for interpretation. As
noted earlier (1.4), it is plausible to suppose that those who

---

of punishment is to 'annul the false evidence seemingly provided by the
wrongdoing of the relative worth of the victim and the wrongdoer' ('A New
Theory of Retribution', 403). Clearly, then, on this account the act to be
annulled is an unfitting act.

[11] Cf. Iris Murdoch, *The Sovereignty of Good* (London, 1970), 77.

are owed justice are superior to those who are not. A refusal to rectify a past injustice, then, may not merely leave untouched the effects of that injustice—may not merely leave the earlier injustice to stand—but may compound the injustice by once again treating those denied justice as less than they are. If this is the argument for the claim that rectification of past injustice is required as a matter of justice, then the argument relies on understanding justice as a member of the fittingness family of concepts.

So far I have considered only annulment arguments for punishment. Do such arguments apply also to rewards? If we accept that punishment will annul wrongdoing, must we also accept that rewarding will annul rightdoing? If so, would this be a reason not to reward? Or should a reluctance to accept that rewards can annul give us reason to doubt that punishment can annul?

We do not usually suppose that rewards are able to annul, though the suggestion may not be as implausible or as unattractive as it may first appear. An argument for rewarding based on annulment may seem implausible for it may seem incompatible with a desire not to undo the past where there has been a right action. But such an objection is, of course, unfounded. Even if punishment is able to annul, it does not undo the past. There is no reason to suppose that accepting an annulment defence of rewards carries the implication that to reward is to undo the action rewarded, in the sense of making it as if the rewarded action was never performed. Nor do arguments for the rectificatory capacity of punishment aim to show that the wrongness of what was originally done can be annulled by punishment. To punish is not supposed to make the original action any less wrong; thus there is no reason to suppose that to accept a parallel argument in the case of rewards would be to accept that a reward makes the original action any less right. These are not reasons, then, to resist the claim that rewarding can annul.

Nevertheless, to make an annulment argument for rewarding right actions we must be able to point to something about a right action which there might be reason to annul. But that there is something is not wholly implausible, and it is possible, in principle at least, to construct parallel arguments to those offered by Morris and Hampton to justify rewards. Morris's argument presupposes that those who do not offend bear a burden of restraint. We might, then, try to argue that those who perform actions worthy of reward bear a burden in undertaking such actions, and it is this which the reward is supposed to annul. In Hampton's argument the function of punishment is to annul the false message of superiority of wrongdoer over victim. Perhaps, then, we may argue that the function of a reward is to annul a false message of superiority of beneficiary over benefactor. No doubt such arguments will face severe difficulties, particularly if they are supposed to be arguments showing that only rewards can annul. But the possibility of annulment arguments for rewards should not be dismissed out of hand. If for no other reason, such arguments are worthy of consideration for the light they shed on annulment arguments for punishment: if we wish to accept an annulment argument for punishments but not for rewards we should be able to explain why one succeeds where the other fails. Certainly it is not obvious that there is nothing about a right action which we should wish a reward to annul.

I turn now to non-rectification approaches to justifying the claim that a failure to punish or reward can be unjust. One such approach focuses on the expressive or communicative capacity of punishment and reward. Punishing and rewarding are ways of treating, ways of giving expression to beliefs, and the use of punishing and rewarding may be viewed as the use of a (particular) language. Thus, it may be argued, the peculiar appropriateness of punishing and rewarding for treating wrongdoers as wrongdoers, rightdoers as rightdoers is to be explained as largely a matter of simple convention. Languages, it may be said, are (very largely) a matter of convention; and it makes little sense to ask for a justification for the adoption of any particular sign. Hence, if the practices of punishing and rewarding are (part of) a language, they too are simply the conventional ways by which (at least in many societies) wrongdoers are treated as wrongdoers, rightdoers as rightdoers. As such no further justification is required.[12] Alternatively, we might claim that it is part of the nature of a language that it is (normally) understood, that use of a language presupposes that effective communication (normally) occurs, and argue that punishment is the only language wrongdoers understand, that only rewards effectively communicate commendation.[13]

But these arguments seem unimpressive. The argument from conventionality is vulnerable to the objection that if another convention could be adopted which did not involve the deliberate infliction of suffering, or the opportunity costs associated with rewarding, then, other things being equal at least, that other convention should be adopted and punishing and rewarding discontinued. It is hard to see how mere convention can be a basis on which to fail to discharge the general duty not to make suffer, and not to deny benefits. The argument from effective communication faces both empirical and non-empirical objections. It is plausible to suppose that, at least for many people, it is simply not true that only punishments and rewards are an effective means of communication. In their case, at least this defence of the necessity of punishment and reward must fail. But even where punishment and reward are the only effective means of communication it is not clear that punishing and rewarding are required for justice, for it is not clear that effective communication is required for justice (as against moral education, say).

These arguments focus on the treatment of the person punished or rewarded. An alternative strategy is to argue that a failure to punish or reward is unjust in view of the way some other person is treated, most plausibly the victim or beneficiary. The argument from the protection of victims is an argument of this type. Punishing, or threatening to punish (and then punishing to ensure that the threat remains credible), is

---

[12] This argument is offered in A. C. Ewing, *The Morality of Punishment*, (London, 1929), 105, and is criticized in C. W. K. Mundle, 'Punishment and Desert', in Acton (ed.), *The Philosophy of Punishment*, 69.

[13] Cf. Igor Primoratz, 'Punishment as Language', *Philosophy*, 64 (1989), 199–200.

a means by which potential victims may be protected, and a failure so to protect, the argument might go, is a failure to treat as valuable, as worthy of protection. As such the argument exhibits the form required by justice as fittingness: failure to protect, if it is unjust, fails to treat those unprotected as worthy of protection; but to be worthy of protection is to have a certain status, and thus a failure to protect people worthy of protection is to treat them as less than they are.[14] (A comparable argument for rewards might be constructed on the basis that potential beneficiaries must be treated as having interests worthy of promotion if they are not to be treated as less than they are. Thus a failure to offer a reward might, in some circumstances, constitute unjust treatment of potential beneficiaries.)

Even if we assume that there is a satisfactory connection between (level of) status and (degree of) protection or assistance, there are a number of difficulties which must be dealt with if such an argument is to succeed in showing that a failure to punish or reward is unjust. Firstly, it must be shown that punishment or reward is necessary, in practice if not in principle, and not merely sufficient, for protection or assistance. Secondly, the argument for punishing, at least, is vulnerable to the charge that in punishing to protect others, those who are punished are treated as only a means, not as ends in themselves. I will return to this line of objection later (6.3).

Thirdly, the arguments presuppose that there is a duty to protect or assist, for unless there is such a duty it is not clear that a failure (to threaten) to punish, or (to offer) to reward treats potential victims or beneficiaries as unworthy of protection or assistance rather than simply fails to treat them at all. There are two ways to overcome this problem: to argue for a general duty on all to protect or assist; or to argue that some are in a special position such that a failure to punish or reward will, in their case, be unjust. To support the latter view

---

[14] See Hampton, 'A New Theory of Retribution', 410–13. Hampton suggests that this argument attempts 'to capture and explain . . . Hegel's idea that punishment in some sense "annuls" crime' (413). But it seems more plausible to view this argument as non-rectificatory.

it is necessary to explain who is in this special position, and why. Mere ability to punish or reward seems not to generate any special responsibility: can does not imply ought. A more plausible claim is that those who bar the use of punishment or rewards by others may incur a responsibility to punish or reward those who wrong those whom they have forbidden to punish or assist those whom they have forbidden to reward. (Thus parents who bar the use of punishment by their children, or states which forbid their citizens from punishing, may thereby acquire a responsibility to punish if they are not to act unjustly.) Why might this be so?

Suppose the state under which I live forbids me from punishing those who assail me, and then refuses to punish my assailants.[15] Am I thereby treated unjustly by the state? Perhaps not. If my assailants are not really wrongdoers, or if it is wrong to punish wrongdoers, then the state will not act unjustly when it does not punish. But if we may suppose that it is understood that my assailants are wrongdoers, and that it is not wrong to punish wrongdoers (non-excessively), then what meaning is to be attached to the action of barring me from punishing, while also failing to impose punishment on my assailants? In these circumstances it may be plausible to say that in so acting the state treats me as a being to whom such actions may (not improperly) be done with impunity. If I am not such a being, and if in being so treated I am treated as less than I am, then by combining the forbidding of punishment with a failure to arrange for punishment, the state treats me unjustly. For those who forbid others to punish, then, it may be that failure to punish is unjust. On this account what makes punishment the required treatment for wrongdoers is that it is punishment which has been barred.

These are, then, some of the arguments which might be offered for the claim that we may act unjustly by failing to punish or reward. The more plausible arguments seem to be those which seek to show that punishment is a means

---

[15] Whether I can be so forbidden without being wronged I shall not consider; whatever view we take on that issue the question of whether the barring agency is required by justice to punish still arises.

uniquely able to annul prior injustice, and the argument that those who bar others from punishing thereby incur an obligation to punish on pain of treating unjustly those whom they bar from punishing. I do not claim that any of these arguments will turn out to be successful. But I do want to suggest that they are consistent with understanding unjust treatment as unfitting.

6.3 The Justice of Punishing and Rewarding

I want now to consider when we will act unjustly by punishing and rewarding, and whether this injustice is compatible with viewing justice as a member of the fittingness family of concepts. Clearly, to punish the innocent or reward the unworthy is unjust; it is unjust because it is to treat them as other than they are—as wrongdoers or rightdoers when they are not. This may not be the only reason why it is unjust. Another reason which will often apply derives from the fact that to punish the innocent usually—though not always— wrongly treats the person punished as a liar, for in many cases innocent people assert their innocence. Nevertheless, it is the fact that to punish is to treat as a wrongdoer, to reward to treat as a rightdoer, which provides the explanation of why punishing the innocent, and rewarding the unworthy, is obviously, always, and by its nature, unjust.

Given the difficulties involved in showing that rewards and punishments are required as a matter of justice we may, then, be inclined to take the view that rewarding and punishing are discretionary practices, that although we may act unjustly if we punish or reward, a failure to reward or punish will never be unjust. On this view, although punishing the innocent or rewarding the unworthy is unjust, as far as (non-comparative) justice is concerned, punishing wrongdoers and rewarding rightdoers is permitted but not required.

As we saw earlier (2.2), this position can be set out in terms of desert. If punishment and reward are discretionary, then they are never deserved. On the Kleinigian account people who have no deserts cannot be treated unfittingly no matter how they are treated. However, it does not follow from the fact that someone does not deserve to be rewarded or punished that they have no (relevant) deserts at all. Those who are innocent of the right- or wrongdoing in question deserve to be treated as such, that is, they deserve not to be rewarded or punished. And if they are not treated in accordance with these deserts, they will be treated unfittingly. By contrast rightdoers and wrongdoers do not merely not deserve rewards or punishments—the consequence of these practices being discretionary—they also do not deserve not to be rewarded or punished. Thus in their case neither rewarding nor failing to reward, neither punishing nor failing to punish, is unjust.

On the Sverdlikian account we can be treated unjustly even if we have no deserts, by being treated as having deserts we do not have. Given that rewarding and punishing are discretionary, rightdoers and wrongdoers do not deserve to be rewarded and punished. But it does not follow that to reward rightdoers or punish wrongdoers is unjust, for if rewarding and punishing are indeed discretionary and thus never actually deserved, then to reward or punish is not to treat as deserving the reward or punishment. Rather, strictly, to reward or punish is to treat as not deserving not to be rewarded or punished. Thus it is not true, even on the Sverdlikian account, that no one ever deserving a reward or punishment entails that rewarding or punishing are always unjust.

The view that punishing and rewarding are discretionary practices has its attractions. One advantage of this position is that it allows us to accommodate the belief that justice and mercy are not in fundamental conflict. If wrongdoers deserve punishment, and an injustice is done if they do not get the punishment they deserve, then, it seems, the exercise of mercy must lead to injustice: to exercise mercy is to fail to give the punishment deserved. To avoid this clash it is necessary to show that, when punishment is deserved, but mercy is exercised, not punishing is not unjust. It is difficult to see how this can be done for it seems to require that, when mercy is due, it is due as a matter of justice. (If we could show this, we might argue that the wrongdoer deserves, or would have deserved, punishment, but also deserves mercy, and the latter outweighs the former.) But if it is a matter of justice that a person be treated with mercy then, it seems, that person is done a wrong if mercy is denied. If mercy is required as a matter of justice, then the recipient has a claim to the merciful treatment. But this is problematic for it is part of the nature of merciful treatment that it is treatment to which the recipient has no claim. Thus either the merciful treatment is treatment the recipient cannot claim, in which case the exercise of mercy leads inevitably to injustice; or the treatment can be claimed, and it is therefore not mercy.

Does it matter if mercy is unjust, or at least leads inevitably to injustice? Should we, perhaps, simply accept that mercy is inevitably unjust, but nevertheless sometimes justified? This would be odd. The notion that we may sometimes be faced with tragic choices, and choices between the exercise of the different virtues, is familiar enough. But it would be puzzling indeed if, by their very nature, the virtues of justice and mercy—two virtues which are not only closely associated in our moral thought, but which we expect to be exercised by all wise judges—were contradictory. And it is hard to see how any virtue could survive being found to be, in its nature, contrary to justice.

The problem posed by mercy is avoided, however, if we reject retributivism and the claim that wrongdoers deserve punishment, and say only that wrongdoers do not deserve not to be punished. In this case we may say that mercy is exercised when someone who does not deserve not to be punished is not punished but is still treated as not deserving not to be punished. This position has its attractions, but it is not without difficulties. As I have noted, it is clearly unjust to punish the innocent and to reward the unworthy. But it may also be argued that to punish wrongdoers is to treat them unjustly if such punishment constitutes being treated as a means only, and not as an end.

The problem here arises from the need to find a justification for punishment, and the difficulties involved in showing that punishment is required in order to treat wrongdoers as wrongdoers. Once we accept that punishing is not necessary in order to treat a person as a wrongdoer, then, it seems, any justification of punishment must focus on some other purpose which is served by the infliction of punishment. The most familiar purpose is deterrence. We punish so as to deter the wrongdoer, and others, in order to reduce wrongdoing and hence suffering in the future. Or we may focus on the victim. We might argue, as we have seen, that punishment is necessary in order to reassert the status of the victim. It seems that some argument of this type is required to rebut the charge that punishment involves suffering and is, therefore, other things being equal, to be avoided. But if either of these are our justification for punishing, then it seems that in choosing to punish—rather than to treat as a wrongdoer by some other means—we are using the wrongdoer simply as a means to bring about our objective.

The injustice of treating people simply as a means is an injustice which exhibits transparently the form which justice as fittingness requires all injustice to have. Being an end is status-affecting: beings which are ends in themselves have a status superior to beings which are not, and which may be used simply as a means or a tool without injustice. Why is being an end status-affecting? We may distinguish between two senses in which a being may be viewed as an end: as having a will and being able to act; and as having a good or interests of its own. We usually suppose ourselves to be ends in both senses: as agents and authors of actions we view ourselves as the ends of explanatory chains, as unmoved movers; and as beings with interests we view ourselves as the ends of evaluative chains, the promotion of our interests we suppose to be intrinsically, and not merely instrumentally, good. (It may be that a being has interests if and only if it is able to act, but if so this needs to be shown: the two notions are distinct, and it would seem that we usually suppose that a being, a young infant, say, can have interests without having the capacity to act.) Since we suppose that a being which is free and rational is superior to one which is not, and that a being which has a good of its own is superior to one which has not, we suppose that being an end is superior to being that which is only a means or a tool, and may appropriately be used as such, to being an entity which is neither capable of action nor has interests of its own.

If we treat people without regard either for their interests, or to their will, we will risk treating them simply as tools, simply as a means to whatever end we are pursuing. If those whom we treat are ends, then such treatment is unfitting. To avoid this charge we must either respect the will of the being we treat, or, as when we act paternalistically, we must argue that we are acting in a manner which will promote the being's interests. (Paternalism may be unfitting, but not because those whose liberty is restricted are treated as simply a means.)

These points can be applied to the justification of punishment. We will not be treating as only a means if in punishing we respect the will of the person punished (if the person punished can be said to have chosen or consented to be punished), or if punishment is restricted to cases where it is in the interests of the person punished. The problem is, of course, that these conditions are very restrictive, being satisfied on only some of the occasions on which many suppose punishment to be defensible and not unjust. It may be possible to broaden the scope of these conditions by arguing either that rational, albeit hypothetical, choice or consent to be punished respects the will of the person punished, and that all or most can be deemed to have so chosen; or that a system of punishment is defensible if it supplies benefits (in the form of protection, say) to all, including those who are punished, where those benefits outweigh the cost of punishment to each individual, and cannot be supplied (given that we exclude, say, arrangements which fail to treat all as equals) without imposing the punishment in question. (To the extent that these arguments are not available in the case where punishment would be of the innocent there is reason to suppose that the punishment of the innocent is unjust not only because it treats the innocent as wrongdoers, but because it fails to treat the innocent as ends in themselves.) It may also be possible to argue that, at least to some degree, the charge that we are treating people as a means only can be rebutted if the end (say, protection) is to some degree sacrificed in order to promote the interests of the person punished.

There are, clearly, problems in sustaining such arguments, but I will not pursue them here.[16] My aim has been, not to show whether or when punishing wrongdoers is just, but only that justice as fittingness is the way to think about this issue. The argument against punishing from the requirement to treat people as ends in themselves is entirely consistent with justice as fittingness. Whether it can be met is not a question on which the defence of justice as fittingness relies.

In general there is no comparable problem with rewards. If we insist on rewarding someone—in order to encourage others, say—where receipt of the reward was contrary to the interests and wishes of the recipient, by rewarding we could be said to be using the person rewarded. But rewards are usually supposed to promote the interests of recipients, and recipients are usually supposed to be free to decline rewards if they so wish. Thus rewarding rarely involves the risk of treating the recipient as only a means.

I set out in this chapter to see whether the arguments for and against the justice of rewarding and punishing, and of failing to reward and punish, fit the pattern which justice as fittingness dictates. I have not, of course, considered all the arguments which may be offered on these two questions. But I have tried to illustrate the forms which arguments on these issues might take. I do not want to claim that any of these arguments are successful. But what I do claim is that they follow the pattern required if justice is to be a member of the fittingness family of concepts.

I have also sought to establish whether, if we accept justice as fittingness, we must also accept that the practices of rewarding and punishing must play a significant role in any

[16] For a detailed discussion of this issue, see Richard W. Burgh, 'Punishment and Respect for Persons', doctoral thesis, University of Wisconsin, 1975.

just society. The arguments we have considered have not shown this to be so. While viewing justice as a fittingness concept is compatible with retributivism (indeed retributivism may presuppose that justice is a fittingness concept), we may accept justice as fittingness and reject retributivism.

7

Desert and Responsibility

In this chapter I examine the relationship between desert and responsibility. As I noted earlier (2.3), the view that to be deserving we must be responsible for that which makes us deserving, taken with a belief that we are, in the end, responsible for very little, has been a significant contributing factor to the revolt against desert. The primary objective of this chapter is to argue against this view, and thus to defend the claim that justice is to be understood as treating in accordance with desert.

I argue that the claim that we can deserve only on the basis of that for which we are responsible—the desert-responsibility thesis—is false, and that there is no conceptual connection between desert and responsibility. However, it is certainly true that many claims to deserve are undermined if there is a lack of responsibility. Were this not so the desert-responsibility thesis could not have attracted the support which it has. Thus I seek to explain why it is that a lack of responsibility can sometimes, *but only sometimes*, undermine a desert claim, and to distinguish those cases where a lack of responsibility undermines a claim to deserve from those where it does not. I consider three accounts of the distinction between desert claims which do, and desert claims which do not, presuppose responsibility, endorsing an account which explains the distinction as arising from the mode of treatment supposed to be deserved.

7.1 *Counter-examples to the Desert-Responsibility Thesis*

It is often supposed that there is a relationship between desert and responsibility: that to be deserving we must be responsible for that which makes us deserving.[1] This supposed relationship between desert and responsibility, combined with a growing tendency to view less and less as the responsibility of the individual, has been a significant source of the reluctance to appeal to desert which has been a feature of much recent moral and political philosophy.[2] Certainly, if to be deserving we need to be responsible for that which makes us deserving 'all the way down',[3] it is not easy to see how anyone could ever be deserving of anything.

I want to reject the desert-responsibility thesis. We may see that the thesis is false by considering a number of (types of)

---

[1] For example, Sadurski writes: 'It makes no sense to attribute desert, positive or negative, to persons for actions or facts over which they have no control' (Wojciech Sadurski, *Giving Desert its Due* (Dordrecht, 1985), 117) and later: 'If we cannot ascribe responsibility, we cannot talk of desert' (ibid. 131); Glover suggests that we call 'desert-based' those attitudes which are 'linked to responsibility, such as pride, guilt, resentment, gratitude, and some sorts of regret' (Jonathan Glover, 'Self-Creation', *Proceedings of the British Academy*, 69 (1983), 466); and Lamont claims that 'one of the defining characteristics of desert . . . is that it does require some minimum degree of voluntariness' (Julian Lamont, 'The Concept of Desert in Distributive Justice', *Philosophical Quarterly*, 44 (1994), 53).

The alternative view is put by Galston, in a passage he describes as summarizing the 'major findings' of 'recent scholarship' on desert: 'Desert-related facts need not themselves be deserved—earned, merited, achieved through effort. They may, to use Rawls' phrase, be "arbitrary from a moral point of view", in that there is no moral reason why individual A rather than B should be characterized by a desert-related fact. But this does not mean that these amoral facts cannot be the basis of moral claims' (William A. Galston, *Justice and the Human Good* (Chicago, 1980), 172).

[2] An impressive case for this claim is made by Samuel Scheffler, who argues that 'the reluctance of many contemporary political philosophers to rely on a pre-institutional notion of desert results in part from a widespread, though often implicit skepticism about individual agency, a form of skepticism which is the contemporary descendant of skepticism about freedom of the will' (Samuel Scheffler, 'Responsibility, Reactive Attitudes, and Liberalism in Philosophy and Politics', *Philosophy and Public Affairs*, 21 (1992), 309–10).

[3] Robert Nozick, *Anarchy, State and Utopia* (Oxford, 1974), 225.

counter-examples. One set of counter-examples arises from what we might call fundamental facts about a being. Most human beings are, we suppose, free and rational; rats and beetles, we think, are neither free nor rational. Let us assume we are correct in our ascriptions of freedom and rationality. Now suppose it is objected that rats and beetles are not responsible for being non-rational and unfree, and that they do not, therefore, deserve to suffer as a consequence. Similarly, the argument goes, we cannot claim to deserve any particular treatment on the basis of being free and rational, for we cannot claim to be responsible for being free and rational. Such arguments, I take it, are not persuasive. Free and rational beings deserve to be treated as such—and their being deserving of such treatment is in no way undermined by any lack of responsibility for being free and rational. In such cases the question of responsibility simply does not arise.

Secondly, consider the case of competitions. We may speak of a competitor as deserving or not deserving victory. The team which plays best (on the day) deserves to win. If luck or a bad refereeing decision prevent this, then the moral victor does not receive what is due. (The best player on the day—the player who actually plays best—may not be the best player *simpliciter*. Steffi Graf may be the best player, but if she is having an off day and plays badly, then she does not deserve to win.) But in judging whether competitors deserve to win we do not consider whether, or to what extent, they are responsible for possessing those attributes which enable them to win. Of course, many competitions require effort and training by anyone who wishes to have any hope of success. But if a player out-performs all others simply on the basis of natural talent, then that player deserves to win.[4]

----

[4] Cf.: 'When we say the prettiest girl deserves to win the beauty contest, the most skilful shot deserves to win at marbles, the ablest candidate deserves the scholarship, we look no further than the present qualities of the individuals concerned' (David Miller, *Social Justice* (Oxford, 1976), 96–7). Broadly speaking this seems to be true, although, as we have seen, we would not say that the most skilful shot deserved to win if this skill was not exhibited in the particular game. (A similar point applies to the beauty contest, if beauty can wax and wane.) And, if we are concerned with deserving *to win*

Finally, consider cases where that which deserves is not a person. As I suggested earlier (2.1), there seems no doubt that non-persons can deserve. Equally there seems no doubt that non-persons are not, indeed cannot be, responsible for the basis on which they deserve. But if desert presupposes responsibility, how can it be that what cannot be responsible can deserve?

These examples confirm that the desert-responsibility thesis is false: not all desert claims presuppose a responsibility on the part of the deserver; at most only some do. But if that is so, what is it that distinguishes those desert claims which presuppose responsibility from those which do not? I want to consider three accounts which try to answer this question.

7.2 *The Moral/Non-moral Desert Distinction Account*

The first account relies on drawing a distinction between moral and non-moral uses of 'desert'. Armed with this distinction we are, so the argument goes, able to explain why some, though only some, desert claims presuppose responsibility: it is not that *desert* presupposes responsibility, it is that *moral* desert, and only *moral* desert, presupposes responsibility. For the sake of the argument I will assume that there are indeed moral and non-moral uses of 'desert'. I do not, myself, wish to endorse such a distinction, and I shall not attempt to spell out how the supposed distinction might be drawn; rather I shall assume that an intuitive understanding is sufficient to enable us to judge whether this alleged distinction is likely to

the scholarship, then again the abilities must be exhibited. It may be that the most able candidate deserves the scholarship, but if that candidate has an off day when the competitive examination is held, then we should not say that that candidate deserved to win. It might be suggested that we do 'look further' than present qualities, for the unfair acquisition of a putative desert basis will undermine the claim to deserve. (Cf. Lamont, 'The Concept of Desert in Distributive Justice', 48). However, it may be that, rather than unfair acquisition undermining a desert basis, unfair acquisition generates a countervailing desert claim which simply outweighs the original: where we acquire an attribute unfairly we do not simply not deserve to benefit from it, we deserve not to benefit from it.

prove useful in any attempt to distinguish those cases where a lack of responsibility undermines a desert claim from those where it does not.

How well does the account explain why desert is not undermined by a lack of responsibility in the examples we have just considered? Consider fundamental facts about a deserver. Some claims of this type do seem to involve a moral use of 'desert': we might say that all people are free agents, or are sentient beings, and deserve to be treated as such. Such claims may be false—that is not the issue. The question is whether they must be non-moral uses of 'desert', and there seems no reason to say that they must. Indeed these uses seem to be among the prime candidates for inclusion in any category of *moral* desert.

What of competitive desert? When we say that a particular baby deserves to win the baby competition, or the team which outplays its opponent deserves to win the contest, are we making a non-moral use of 'desert'? At best this seems unclear. In cases where people believe their team, or the contestant they support, deserved to win, failure to win may lead to claims that 'there is no justice', or that their team or contestant 'was robbed'. On the face of it these are not amoral complaints. They suggest that, when 'desert' is used in the context of competitions, it is, at least sometimes, a moral use of 'desert'.

Finally, what of non-personal desert? At first sight it might seem that this account can explain why the impossibility of responsibility does not preclude there being such desert: non-personal desert does not presuppose responsibility because it is always non-moral desert, and it is only moral desert which presupposes responsibility. But is non-personal desert always non-moral desert? Suppose an environmentalist asserts that the Tasmanian wilderness deserves to be protected and preserved—not for reasons of prudence, but for its own sake. Is it clear that this cannot be a moral use of 'desert'? Again the issue is not whether such a putatively moral claim is true, but whether it can be made. It is, to say the least, controversial to claim that it cannot, or that such a statement could not be a moral use of 'desert'.

I conclude, then, that this account is a failure: the distinction between moral and non-moral uses of 'desert' (even if we could make out such a distinction) seems not to correspond to the distinction between cases of desert which presuppose responsibility and cases which do not.

7.3 The Attribute Requirement Account

The second account I want to consider begins from the requirement noted earlier (2.1) that the desert basis must be a fact about the deserver. If this is granted, it becomes possible to argue that a lack of responsibility is able to subvert a desert claim by undermining the presupposition that the (would-be) desert basis may properly be said to be a fact about the (would-be) deserver. Lack of responsibility, we might argue, undermines desert by severing the vital link between the (would-be) deserver and the fact which would, but for the lack of responsibility, function as the desert basis. I will call such an explanation the 'attribute requirement account'.

How does this process—this severing—occur? The idea here is that a lack of responsibility will preclude any inferences about a person's true self. We draw a distinction between what people do—their actions, for which they are responsible—and what happens to them. We can, at least in general, infer facts about people from what they do, but not, usually, from what merely happens to them.[5] If I believe you have deliberately trodden on my foot, I may infer that you are violent and malicious, and believe you to be deserving of censure. But if I believe that you have inadvertently and non-negligently trodden on my foot, I shall think of this as something which has happened to you. It is not something which you have done, and thus, usually, it is not something from which I may make inferences about you. A comparable argument might be offered for aspects of character. Suppose we

---

[5] Cf.: 'it is scarcely radical to say that when we are concerned with what a person deserves, we are interested in his behaviour *as a display of character*' (Norvin Richards, 'Luck and Desert', *Mind*, 95 (1986), 200).

think John cannot help being cruel to cats. In that case, so the argument goes, he cannot have deserts on the basis of his cruelty, for acquiring the characteristic of being cruel is something which has happened to John. Being cruel is something associated with John, not something he is in himself.[6] It is, then, plausible to view as associated a lack of responsibility, a failure to provide evidence of facts about the subject, and a lack of desert. A lack of responsibility undermines the claim that the relevant fact is really a fact about the putative deserver (a fact about the putative deserver's real self), and, if the desert basis must be a fact about the deserver, the desert claim itself is undermined.

How successful is this account in explaining why the desert-responsibility thesis does not apply in the cases we identified earlier? It seems most successful in dealing with cases where the desert basis is a fundamental characteristic. If the attribute requirement account is sound, then the plausibility with which a lack of responsibility undermines a particular desert claim will depend upon the plausibility of denying that the putative desert basis is really a fact about the deserver. And we are, we may suppose, very reluctant to deny that fundamental facts are really facts about the putative deserver; and thus it is to be expected that desert is not undermined in such cases, irrespective of responsibility. I may not be responsible for being a free or sentient being, but these characteristics are so fundamental to any conception of me—the argument goes—that it is impossible to regard being free or sentient as features which just happen to have become associated with (the real) me.

---

[6] It has been suggested that an argument of this type is available to Rawls: 'On Rawls' conception, the characteristics I possess do not *attach* to the self but are only *related* to the self, standing always at a certain distance. . . . We can see in this light how Rawls' argument from arbitrariness undermines desert not directly, by claiming I cannot *deserve* what is arbitrarily given, but indirectly, by showing I cannot *possess* what is arbitrarily given, that is, that "I", *qua* subject of possession, cannot possess it in the undistanced, constitutive sense necessary to provide a desert base' (Michael J. Sandel, *Liberalism and the Limits of Justice* (Cambridge, 1982), 85).

What of competitive desert? How can the attribute requirement account explain why we believe that those who deserve to win do so irrespective of whether they are responsible for playing more ably, or for the attributes on which their desert is based? Why should we be reluctant to divorce such behaviour or such attributes from the competitor? Here the account seems less successful: it is not clear how the attribute requirement account can make sense of any particular reluctance to see desert undermined by a lack of responsibility in such cases.

Finally, what of non-personal desert? Here it might be argued that, since there is no possibility of action (in the relevant sense), and hence no distinguishing between what the putative deserver does and what happens to it, there is less impetus to seek to isolate the equivalent of a real self to which things may happen but which remains untouched by them. Thus, the argument goes, it seems less plausible to say that putative facts about a forest, book, or building, and so on are not really facts about the forest, book, or building in itself, and thus there is a tendency to say that such facts cannot function as desert bases.

The attribute requirement account, then, may have *some* success in explaining why the desert-responsibility thesis fails to apply to some cases. But there seems no doubt that it cannot provide a comprehensive account of why some desert claims are undercut by a lack of responsibility and some are not, for, by its nature, it cannot account for cases where (we think) a lack of responsibility undermines a desert claim, but where (we think) the fact which, but for the absence of responsibility, would have been a desert basis is still a fact about the would-be deserver. And it is plausible to suppose that there are such cases. For example, we may wish to argue that a lack of responsibility undermines the claim that John deserves some particular treatment on the basis of his propensity to cruelty, without wanting to claim that John is not really cruel, does not really have that propensity. And this the account cannot explain.

The underlying problem here—which ought to make us wonder whether, even when this account provides the right answer, it provides it for the right reason—is that, for many, the notion that desert presupposes responsibility is simply more plausible than are the premises of this attempt to account for it. The notion that there are real or transcendent selves which, in some way, come to have certain properties contingently associated with them is a possible way of thinking. We may suppose that John is not really cruel to cats—that is, the real John is not cruel to cats he merely has cruelness to cats associated with him. But being a possible description is not enough. We need to be willing to think of this description as the most reasonable description if this is to be the source of our readiness to believe that a lack of responsibility undermines desert. And surely for many of us that is just not so. Our preferred description may be that John is cruel to cats, and the propensity to be cruel to cats *is* a fact about John. He may not be responsible for having such a propensity; but he is, nevertheless, cruel.[7]

7.4 *The Mode of Treatment Account*

As we saw (2.1), desert is a triadic relation between a deserver, that which is deserved, and desert basis. The attribute requirement account focused on the desert basis. I want now to consider an account which concentrates on what is (said to be) deserved. What is deserved is, normally at least, deserved as a form or mode of treatment: as a punishment, a mark of respect, or some other form. Now some modes of treatment— reward and punishment in particular—presuppose a responsibility on the part of the recipient. There is, therefore, the possibility of explaining why some, but only some, desert claims are undercut if responsibility is absent by arguing that a desert claim will be undermined by a lack of responsibility if, but only if, what is (said to be) deserved is a mode of

---

[7] Cf. George Sher, *Desert* (Princeton, 1987), 157: 'it is perfectly consistent to say that persons are not responsible for having certain characteristics, yet that precisely these characteristics make them the people they are'.

treatment which presupposes responsibility. Further, this account offers the possibility of supplementing the explanation (based on the denial of moral luck) offered earlier (2.1) for the wide acceptance of the desert-responsibility thesis: given a tendency to suppose that *all* desert claims are concerned with responsibility-presupposing modes of treatment we should expect that a lack of responsibility will be thought to undermine desert itself.

The mode of treatment account begins from the claim that some—but only some—deserved modes of treatment presuppose a responsibility on the part of the deserver. Where this is so, to say the treatment is deserved, while denying that the (alleged) deserver is responsible, is to make a conceptual mistake. Consider punishment. It is plausible that to punish people is to treat them as responsible for that which they are punished for. If this is so, then, if people are not responsible, it does indeed follow that they cannot deserve to be punished. But it is not that they cannot *deserve* punishment; rather that they cannot deserve *punishment*.[8]

A comparable argument applies in the case of reward. To give a reward, it seems, is to acknowledge responsibility.[9]

---

[8] Cf.: 'It would seem that there are some things like rewards and punishments which, to be deserved, presuppose the responsibility of the person concerned. However, we would not be justified in generalizing this to cover all deserts' (John Kleinig, *Punishment and Desert* (The Hague, 1973), 57–8).

To say that people are treated as if they are responsible is not, of course, to say either that they are responsible, or that they are believed to be so. Where punishment is, intentionally, imposed vicariously or on the basis of strict liability, those who punish may believe that those who are punished are not genuinely responsible for that which they are punished for. Nevertheless, if this is punishment, as against, say, victimization, those punished are treated as if they are responsible.

[9] Brian Barry writes: 'we can only speak of "rewards" and "punishments" where there is voluntary effort involved at some point' (Brian Barry, *Political Argument* (London, 1965), 108). This, no doubt, puts the point too strongly. We may speak of people being punished for their laziness, and laziness requires little in the way of effort—voluntary or otherwise. The issue is one of responsibility, not effort. (And Rawls goes a step further, suggesting that *desert* itself, 'in the ordinary sense', presupposes effort: 'Even the willingness to make an effort, to try, *and so to be deserving in the ordinary sense* is itself dependent upon happy family circumstances' (John Rawls, *A Theory of Justice* (Oxford, 1972), 74, emphasis added).

Rewarding contrasts with praising, admiring, and criticizing, which do not presuppose responsibility.[10] We are restricted in what or who we can give rewards to: while paintings, essays, buildings, machines, and even vegetables can be praised, admired, criticized, and win prizes, none can be rewarded. It is not that the non-responsible cannot *deserve* rewards; it is that they cannot deserve *rewards*. (The higher animals are in some ways hard cases—but it seems not unreasonable to say that, to the extent that we are willing to describe our action as giving a genuine reward, we are supposing the dog, or whatever, to be responsible.)

Other examples of responsibility-presupposing modes of treatment include gratitude and forgiveness. A lack of responsibility will undermine any claim to deserve gratitude or forgiveness: we can be grateful only to those we consider are responsible for our receiving a benefit; we can forgive only those we think are responsible for our injury. Lack of responsibility undermines the possibility of gratitude or forgiveness being deserved. But it is a misleading ellipsis to say of these cases that lack of responsibility has undermined *desert*.

Certain modes of treatment, then, themselves presuppose responsibility. To reward, punish, forgive, show gratitude or resentment, is to presuppose responsibility on the part of the recipient. Such modes express 'reactive attitudes'.[11] Forms of treatment which do not presuppose responsibility include admiring, criticizing, grading, praising, the giving of prizes, the showing of respect, and so on. These forms, by their nature, express appraising rather than reactive attitudes. I am

---

[10] It is striking that throughout his discussion of 'distribution according to desert' (*Giving Desert its Due*, ch. 5), Sadurski, when writing of positive desert, invariably speaks of rewards. However, in a passage where he is concerned with what we deserve on the basis of our 'equal humanness' (ibid. 97), he speaks not of our deserving *to be rewarded* for being (equally) human—which would be odd—but of our deserving respect and concern. It is striking that it is precisely at the point when he is not concerned with reward that Sadurski (implicitly) abandons the view that desert presupposes responsibility.

[11] The term is Strawson's: reactive attitudes are 'essentially reactions to the quality of others' wills' (P. F. Strawson, 'Freedom and Resentment', *Proceedings of the British Academy*, 48 (1962), 199).

not, of course, denying that we may hold responsible those whom we criticize and praise; what I am denying is that we *must* hold responsible those whom we criticize and praise. Criticism and praise do not work like that; punishment and rewards do.

How well does this account allow us to explain why desert is not undermined by a lack of responsibility in the counter-examples to the desert-responsibility thesis? Consider first those based on fundamental characteristics. When we say that people, by virtue of being free and rational, deserve a certain kind of treatment, we are not claiming that such treatment is due *as a reward*. Gods deserve the treatment due to them as gods, but they do not deserve it as a reward. My dog may deserve less favourable treatment than my child, but such treatment is not deserved *as a punishment* for being a dog. Since, in the case of fundamental characteristics, we are not concerned with reward or punishment, or any other responsibility-presupposing mode of treatment, we should not expect a lack of responsibility to undermine desert claims of this type.

I noted earlier (3.3) an example of a fundamental characteristic on the basis of which we may deserve: wholeness. If we are wholes, then we deserve to be treated as such, and that desert is not undermined by any lack of responsibility on our part for being wholes. Even if we are not responsible for being whole, we can, say, deserve to be treated in accordance with our contribution, although, as we saw, we may not deserve to be *rewarded* for our contribution.

What of competitions? Here it is important to distinguish between deserving to win a competition and deserving to win *as a reward*. Lack of responsibility undermines a claim to deserve a reward—and hence a claim to deserve victory as a reward. But it does not undermine a claim to deserve victory *simpliciter*. The most beautiful girl, the most bouncing baby, the tennis player who plays most ably, deserve to win their respective competitions. Responsibility for being beautiful, bouncing, or playing well is irrelevant.[12] If the victory (and

---

[12] Cf.: 'The musical or mathematical prodigy deserves to win the appropriate competition, even if the performance involves no will or choice. In this

accompanying prize) are to be viewed as a reward, then responsibility is relevant. Though we may speak of a particular baby deserving a prize, we could not speak of the baby deserving to be *rewarded* by winning the prize.[13] Only in those cases where there is any plausibility in the claim that the victor is responsible for (at least some of) the virtues, skills, and performance which resulted in victory may we speak of the victory and prize as a deserved reward. In short, then, the desert-responsibility thesis fails to apply in the case of competitions because we may there be concerned only with victory *qua* victory, and prizes *qua* prizes. Only if we view the victory or the prize as a reward will a lack of responsibility undermine the claim to deserve.

Finally, as regards the deserts of non-persons, the deserved modes of treatment never presuppose responsibility. Here there is no will, and hence the reactive attitudes have no place. We cannot punish or reward non-persons. It is to be expected, then, that non-personal desert will be unaffected by the absence of responsibility.

Thus the mode of treatment account seems to offer a plausible explanation of why a lack of responsibility undermines some desert claims but not others. But I want to suggest that this account also helps to explain the intuitive plausibility of the desert-responsibility thesis. Desert can easily seem to presuppose responsibility for it is easy to make the mistake of transferring to the notion of desert what is properly associated only with some of those modes of treatment which can be deserved. The modes of treatment which do presuppose responsibility—in particular, punishing and rewarding—are, after all, a very significant subset of the forms of treatment

respect, there may well be an asymmetry between "positive desert" and punishment' (Galston, *Justice and the Human Good*, 173). There is indeed an asymmetry, though it is not between punishment and (all) 'positive desert'. There is a symmetry between punishing and rewarding, but not between punishing and being victorious.

[13] Here I disagree with Kleinig, who claims that prizes (and honours), in so far as they are deserved, are 'reducible to rewards' (*Punishment and Desert*, 53).

which are said to be deserved. When we think of desert, we tend to think of such notions as punishment and reward.[14]

In addition, there is a tendency to apply the notions of reward and punishment beyond their proper range. It is tempting for recipients of benefits and hardships to speak the language of reward or punishment. By describing benefits as rewards we claim credit for coming to have the basis of our desert. And by describing our hardships as punishments we thereby imply that they are justified only if we are to be held responsible for that which we are being punished for. The description of a hardship as a punishment opens up the possibility of demonstrating that the hardship is unjust on the ground that the recipient is not responsible for what he or she is being punished for. Of course, for each of these arguments there is a complementary argument on the basis of which we might anticipate a reluctance to speak of rewards and punishments: by describing our suffering as a punishment we ascribe discredit for coming to have that basis; to describe a benefit as a reward opens up the possibility of showing it to be unjustified on the grounds that the underlying responsibility claim is not met. To some degree these contrary arguments may apply, and perhaps explain, for example, the popularity of such terms as 'compensation packages' and 'incentives' to describe substantial salaries where beliefs in individual responsibility have been called into question. But the effect of these arguments seems less, perhaps because of the perceived dissimilarities between rewards and punishments. For example, to many it seems churlish to demand much by way of justification for rewards, whereas punishment, being the deliberate imposition of suffering, seems, by its very nature, to call for justification of the very highest standard. At all events if there is a widespread use of reward and punishment in contexts

---

[14] Cf: 'when philosophers themselves make judgements about personal desert, the deserved modes of treatment they have in mind are almost invariably punishment and rewards' (Joel Feinberg, *Doing and Deserving* (Princeton, 1970), 55–6); and 'Contrary to much philosophical opinion, reward and punishment are not the only proper objects of desert' (Kleinig, *Punishment and Desert*, 53).

where desert is attributed, we may expect this, in turn, to result in a tendency to think that all desert presupposes responsibility. That is, a (mistaken) transfer of responsibility from mode of treatment deserved to desert itself may be expected.[15]

The mode of treatment account relies on the claim that certain modes do indeed presuppose responsibility. The claim that reward and punishment presuppose responsibility is hardly controversial, but it may still be asked why, and in what sense, it is so. At one level it may be that no explanation is required beyond making the point that there is a vital difference between those practices which express reactive attitudes and those which do not, and that the terms 'reward' and 'punishment' just happen to be terms we employ to refer to notions which are, in part, characterized by their marking of that important distinction.[16] But a deeper explanation may be available: as I noted earlier (6.1), it is plausible to suppose that punishment and reward are, by their nature, reactions to actions. But actions presuppose responsibility: only if we can be called to (give an) account do we act. Thus to reward or punish is to imply that those who are rewarded or punished are responsible (for that which they are being rewarded or punished for).[17]

[15] Rachels argues: 'Treating people as they deserve is one way of treating them as autonomous beings, responsible for their own conduct. A person who is punished for his misdeeds is *held responsible* for them in a concrete way' (James Rachels, 'What People Deserve', in John Arthur and William H. Shaw (eds.), *Justice and Economic Distribution* (Englewood Cliffs, NJ, 1978), 159). But treating people as they deserve is only sometimes to treat them as autonomous beings. To impose deserved punishment may be to treat as responsible; but that does not show that treatment in accordance with deserts *per se* is to treat as responsible. And it is, surely, this exclusive association of desert with the reactive attitudes that led Glover to suggest 'desert-based' as an appropriate term for such attitudes. But the term is inappropriate: what the reactive attitudes share is not captured by the notion of desert.

[16] That reward and punishment do have this function is consistent with Feinberg's claim that 'punishment is a conventional device for the expression of attitudes of resentment and indignation' (*Doing and Deserving*, 98). As Strawson noted, an attitude of resentment or indignation is appropriate only towards those considered responsible.

[17] We may accept this account of the relation of reward, punishment, and responsibility (and the mode of treatment account as the explanation of the

It seems, then, that the mode of treatment account can explain the distinction we draw between those desert claims which presuppose responsibility and those which do not; and that it is plausible to suppose that the (mistaken) belief that desert itself presupposes responsibility has arisen, at least in part, as a result of desert having been viewed as one of the concepts embodying reactive attitudes. (This, in turn, is to be explained by the association of desert with reward and punishment—concepts which do embody reactive attitudes.) It may be that the use of desert always presupposes an *appraising* attitude. But *reactive* attitudes are no more than a proper subset of appraising attitudes. Given the counter-examples we noted at the outset we may be confident that the desert-responsibility thesis is false; but it is reassuring to have an explanation of how the desert-responsibility thesis can come to seem plausible. And, of course, such an explanation protects us from any seductive attractions of the thesis in the future.

What are the implications of the argument of this chapter for the issue of moral luck? I suggested earlier (2.1) that it is reasonable to suppose that the appeal of the desert-responsibility thesis derives, at least in part, from its association with the denial of moral luck. The view that there is no such thing as moral luck seems plausible.[18] And once we deny the possibility of moral luck it may seem to follow that we cannot deserve on the basis of what we are not responsible for. The argument here relies, as we saw, on the status requirement: if the desert basis must be a basis of appraisal (the

relation between desert and responsibility) without implying that the responsibility required by those desert claims which do presuppose responsibility is any more than that which is required for action. Thus, if we are willing to allow that the existence of action is compatible with determinism, a belief in determinism may be compatible with a belief that people can be responsible in the sense which responsibility-presupposing desert claims require.

[18] Cf.: 'Prior to reflection it is intuitively plausible that people cannot be morally assessed for what is not their fault, or for what is due to factors beyond their control' (Thomas Nagel, *Mortal Questions* (Cambridge, 1979), 25).

status requirement), and if we cannot be appraised on the basis of what we are not responsible for (the denial of moral luck), then that for which we are not responsible cannot function as a desert basis. Thus to be deserving we must be responsible for that which makes us deserving (the desert-responsibility thesis). But if the argument of this chapter is sound, and the desert-responsibility thesis is false, then there must be something wrong with this argument for the desert-responsibility thesis from the denial of moral luck. If the argument is valid, then to reject its conclusion we must reject at least one of its premises. It would seem, then, that if we accept the status requirement we must accept the existence of moral luck.

I have examined the relationship between desert and responsibility since the desert-responsibility thesis seems to have been a primary basis for the reluctance to accept the importance of desert. We have now seen that we cannot dismiss desert on the basis of its presupposing a responsibility we do not have, for desert does not presuppose responsibility. It may be argued that we should reject the notions of reward and punishment on this basis, though if the responsibility required for reward and punishment to be appropriate is no more than that which is required for someone to have acted, then to claim that rewarding and punishing can never be appropriate because we invariably lack the requisite responsibility is to make a controversial claim indeed. It is to be committed not only to the rejection of reward and punishment, but to the rejection of the view that at least some of us, some of the time, are agents, and of all those beliefs which presuppose that this is so.

But even if we do indeed lack responsibility in the sense required for genuine action, and therefore abandon the reactive attitudes and such practices as rewarding, punishing, and the showing of resentment and gratitude, it remains possible to act unjustly. We may act unjustly not only by failing to treat people in accordance with what they do, but in accordance with what they are. We may act unjustly not only by the adoption of unfitting reactive attitudes, but by adopting unfitting non-reactive appraising attitudes: in particular the non-reactive but appraising attitude of respect. People deserve to be treated with appropriate respect, and they may be done an injustice if they are denied the respect they are due.

Afterword

My argument that justice is a member of the fittingness family of concepts is now complete. I shall not attempt to summarize the argument; rather I want to end by noting the work that remains to be done if this account of the concept of justice is to be used to develop a conception of justice, an account of what justice requires. As I noted earlier (1.3), to accept justice as fittingness is to accept that there are two main sources of disagreement over substantive issues of justice.

First, disagreements as to what our actions mean, that is, disagreements in interpretation, feed through into disagreements as to what must be avoided if we are not to act unjustly. I have not attempted here to defend any particular account of how we are to discern the meaning of an action, how we are to determine what an action expresses. But a satisfactory defence of substantive principles of justice must include an account of what counts as treating as a member of a particular category.

Second, disagreements as to what justice requires may reflect disagreements as to which attributes we have, and which attributes are status-affecting. That we are free and rational we generally grant, but are we wholes? At various points in the argument I have done little more than assume that to be reliable, caring, whole, and so on, is to have a superior status. But any thoroughgoing defence of a conception of justice, any particular view of what justice requires, calls for a full account of who we are, and who we should aspire to be.

Bibliographical Details of Works Cited

ACTON, H. B. (ed.), *The Philosophy of Punishment* (London: Macmillan, 1969).

ANSCOMBE, G. E. M., 'Modern Moral Philosophy', *Philosophy*, 33 (1958), 1–19.

—— *The Collected Papers of G. E. M. Anscombe, iii: Ethics, Religion and Politics* (Oxford: Blackwell, 1981).

ARTHUR, JOHN, and SHAW, WILLIAM H. (eds.), *Justice and Economic Distribution,* (Englewood Cliffs, NJ: Prentice-Hall, 1978).

BARNES, JONATHAN, 'Partial Wholes', *Social Philosophy and Policy*, 8 (1990), 1–23.

BARRY, BRIAN, *Political Argument* (London: Routledge & Kegan Paul, 1965).

BURGH, RICHARD W. 'Punishment and Respect for Persons', doctoral thesis, University of Wisconsin, 1975.

—— 'Do the Guilty Deserve Punishment?', *Journal of Philosophy*, 79 (1982), 193–210.

CAMPBELL, T. D., 'Humanity before Justice', *British Journal of Political Science*, 4 (1974), 1–16.

COHEN, G. A., *Karl Marx's Theory of History: A Defence* (Oxford: Oxford University Press, 1978).

COHEN, MARSHALL, NAGEL, THOMAS, and SCANLON, THOMAS (eds.), *Equality and Preferential Treatment* (Princeton: Princeton University Press, 1977).

DELINKO, DAVID, 'Some Thoughts on Retributivism', *Ethics*, 101 (1991), 537–59.

EWIN, R. E., *Co-operation and Human Values* (Brighton: Harvester, 1981).

EWING, A. C. *The Morality of Punishment* (London: Kegan Paul, Trench, Trubner, 1929).

FEINBERG, JOEL, *Doing and Deserving: Essays in the Theory of Responsibility* (Princeton: Princeton University Press, 1970).

FEINBERG, JOEL, *Rights, Justice, and the Bounds of Liberty* (Princeton: Princeton University Press, 1980).

FINNIS, JOHN, *Natural Law and Natural Rights* (Oxford: Clarendon Press, 1980).

FREY, R. G., and MORRIS, CHRISTOPHER (eds.), *Liability and Responsibility: Essays in Law and Morals* (Cambridge: Cambridge University Press, 1991).

GALSTON, WILLIAM A., *Justice and the Human Good* (Chicago: University of Chicago Press, 1980).

GLOVER, JONATHAN, 'Self-Creation', *Proceedings of the British Academy*, 69 (1983), 445–71.

HAYEK, F. A., *Law, Legislation and Liberty, ii: The Mirage of Social Justice* (London: Routledge & Kegan Paul, 1976).

HOFFMAN, JOSHUA, 'A New Theory of Comparative and Noncomparative Justice', *Philosophical Studies*, 70 (1993), 165–83.

HOSPERS, JOHN, *Human Conduct: An Introduction to the Problems of Ethics* (New York: Harcourt Brace, 1961).

KLEINIG, JOHN, 'The Concept of Desert', *American Philosophical Quarterly*, 8 (1971), 71–8.

—— *Punishment and Desert* (The Hague: Martinus Nijhoff, 1973).

LAMONT, JULIAN, 'The Concept of Desert in Distributive Justice', *Philosophical Quarterly*, 44 (1994), 45–64.

LAWRENCE, D. H., *Selected Poems* (Harmondsworth: Penguin, 1950).

LEMMON, E. J., 'Moral Dilemmas', *Philosophical Review*, 71 (1962), 139–58.

LUCAS, J. R., *On Justice* (Oxford: Clarendon Press, 1980).

MILL, J. S., *Utilitarianism*, ed. Mary Warnock, (London: Collins Fontana, 1962).

MILLER, DAVID, *Social Justice* (Oxford: Clarendon Press, 1976).

MONTAGUE, PHILLIP, 'Comparative and Non-comparative Justice', *Philosophical Quarterly*, 30 (1980), 131–40.

MOORE, G. E., *Principia Ethica* (Cambridge: Cambridge University Press, 1903).

MORRIS, HERBERT, 'Persons and Punishment', *Monist*, 52 (1968), 475–501.

MURDOCH, IRIS, *The Sovereignty of Good* (London: Routledge & Kegan Paul, 1970).

NAGEL, THOMAS, *Mortal Questions* (Cambridge: Cambridge University Press, 1979).

NOZICK, ROBERT, *Anarchy, State and Utopia* (Oxford: Basil Blackwell, 1974).

—— *The Examined Life* (New York: Simon & Schuster, 1989).

PARFIT, DEREK, *Reasons and Persons* (Oxford: Clarendon Press, 1984).

PRIMORATZ, IGOR, 'Punishment as Language', *Philosophy*, 64 (1989), 187–205.

QUINTON, ANTHONY, (ed.), *Political Philosophy* (Oxford: Oxford University Press, 1967).

RAWLS, JOHN, *A Theory of Justice* (Oxford: Oxford University Press, 1972).

RICHARDS, NORVIN, 'Luck and Desert', *Mind*, 95 (1986), 198–209.

SADURSKI, WOJCIECH, *Giving Desert its Due* (Dordrecht: Reidel, 1985).

SANDEL, MICHAEL J., *Liberalism and the Limits of Justice* (Cambridge: Cambridge University Press, 1982).

SCHEFFLER, SAMUEL, 'Responsibility, Reactive Attitudes, and Liberalism in Philosophy and Politics', *Philosophy and Public Affairs*, 21 (1992), 299–323.

SCHWARTZ, BARRY, *Vertical Classification* (Chicago: University of Chicago Press, 1981).

SEARLE, JOHN R., *Speech Acts* (London: Cambridge University Press, 1969).

SHER, GEORGE, *Desert* (Princeton: Princeton University Press, 1987).

SKILLEN, A. J., 'How to Say Things with Walls', *Philosophy*, 55 (1980), 509–23.

STERBA, JAMES P., 'Recent Work on Alternative Conceptions of Justice', *American Philosophical Quarterly*, 23 (1986), 1–22.

STRAWSON, P. F. 'Freedom and Resentment', *Proceedings of the British Academy*, 48 (1962), 187–211.

SVERDLIK, STEVEN, 'The Logic of Desert', *Journal of Value Inquiry*, 17 (1983), 317–24.

TEN, C. L., *Crime, Guilt and Punishment* (Oxford: Clarendon Press, 1987).

WARNOCK, GEOFFREY, *The Object of Morality* (London: Methuen, 1971).

WEBER, MAX, H. H. GERTH, and C. WRIGHT MILLS, *From Max Weber: Essays in Sociology*, trans. and ed. (London: Routledge & Kegan Paul, 1970).

Index